This book is belongs to

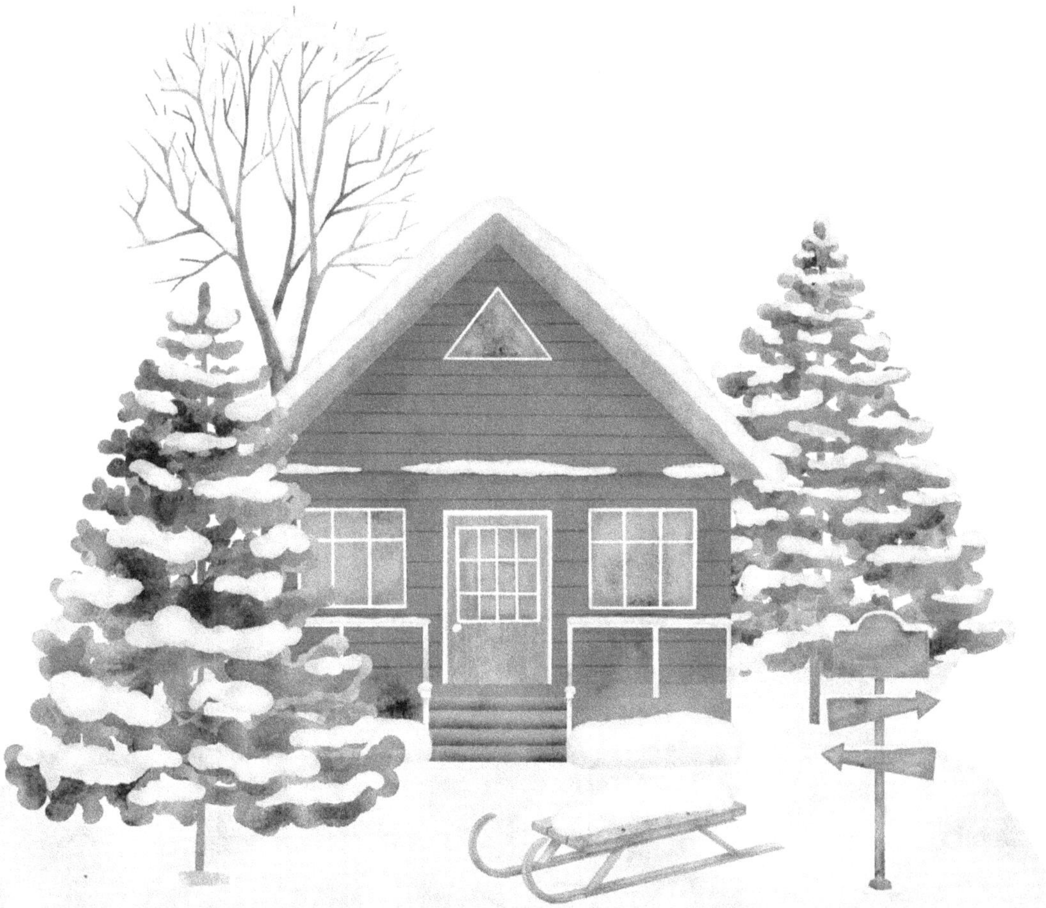

color test page

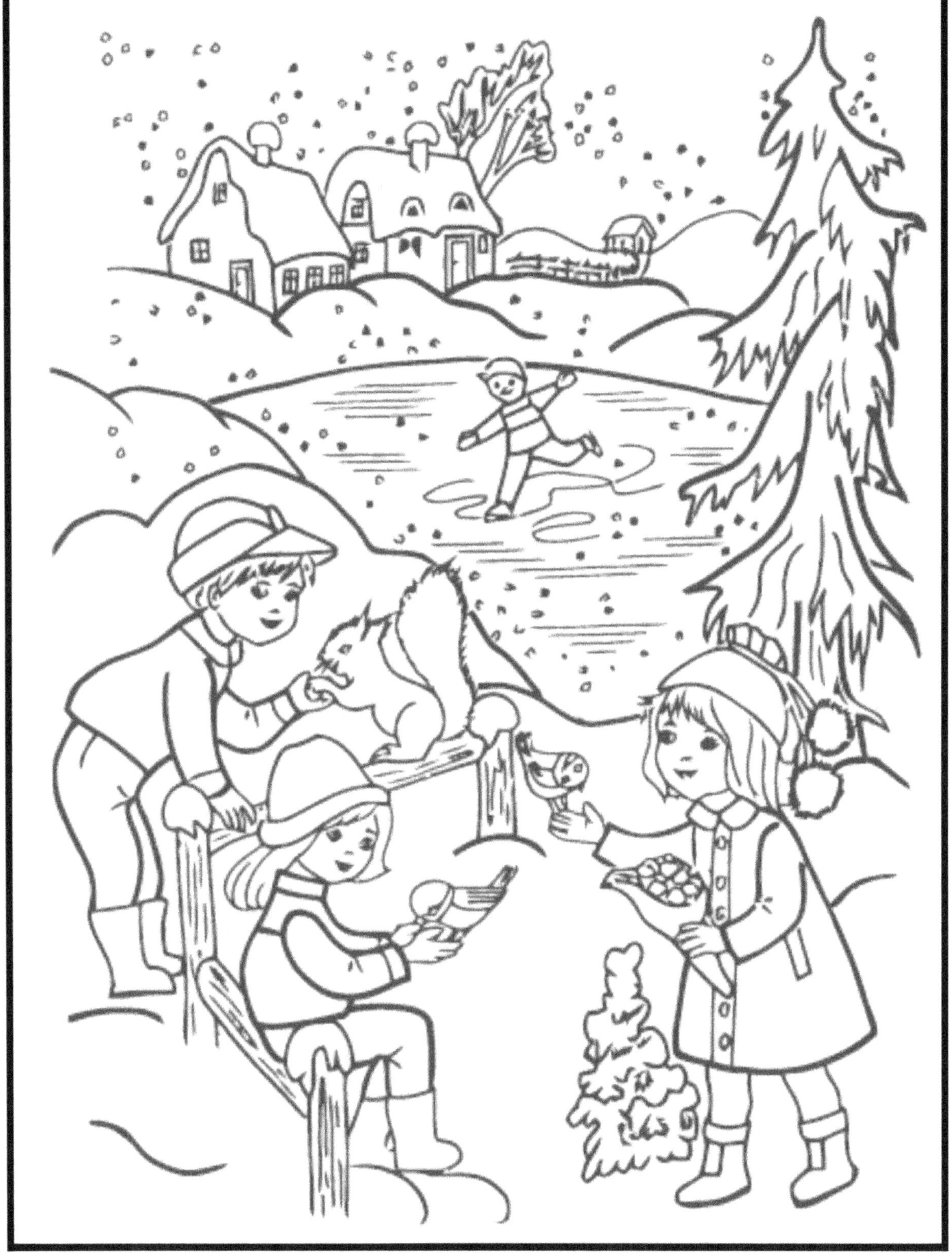

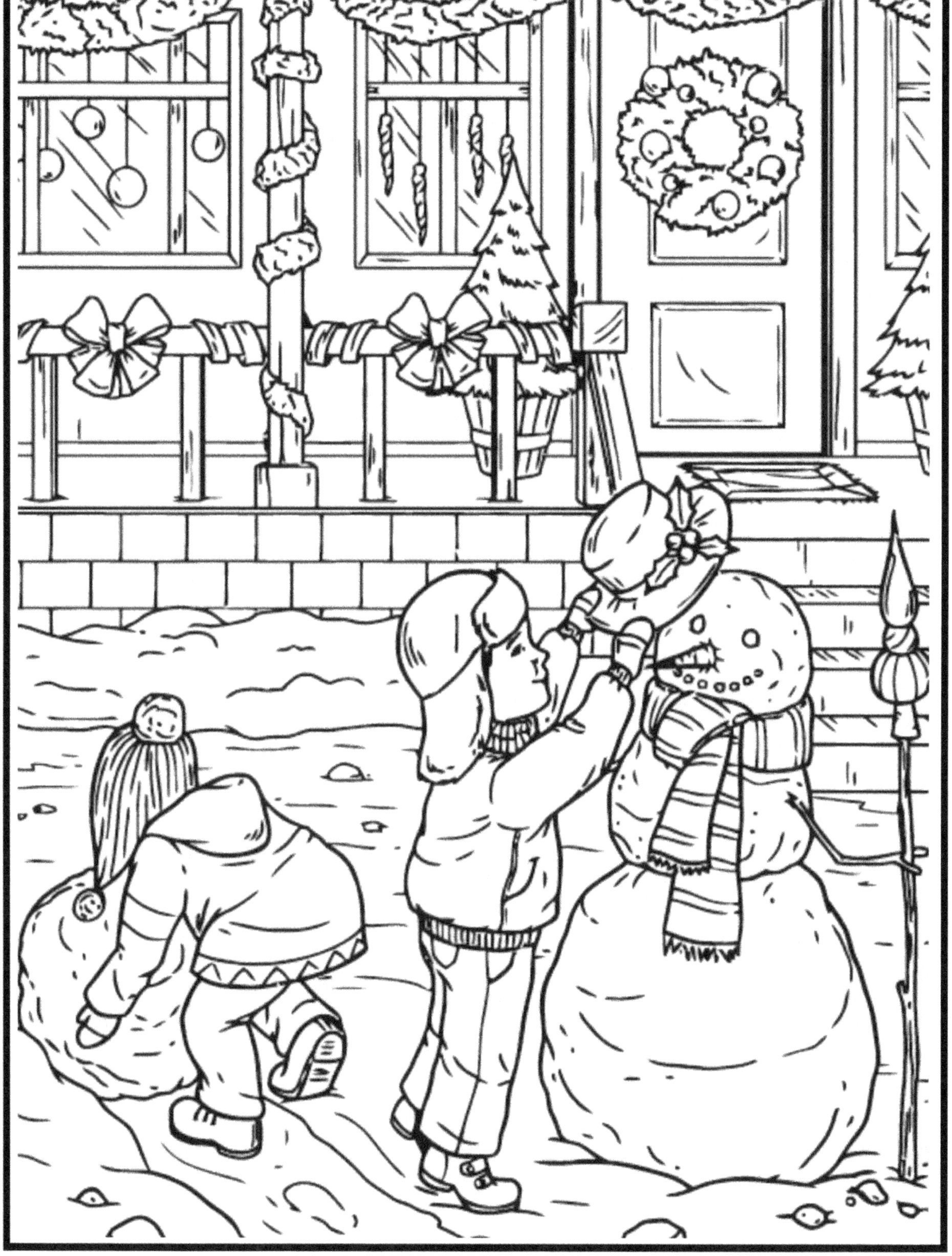

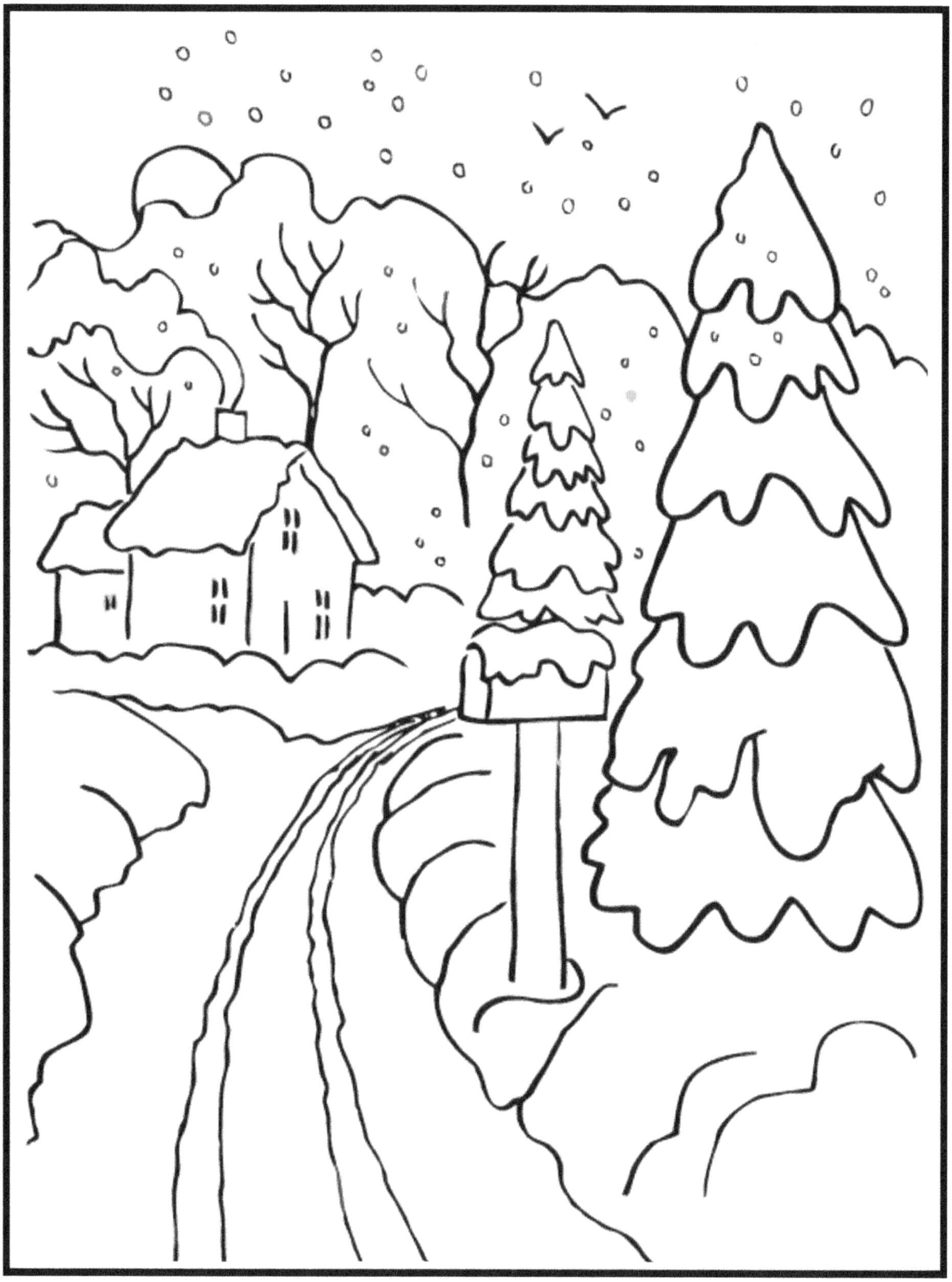

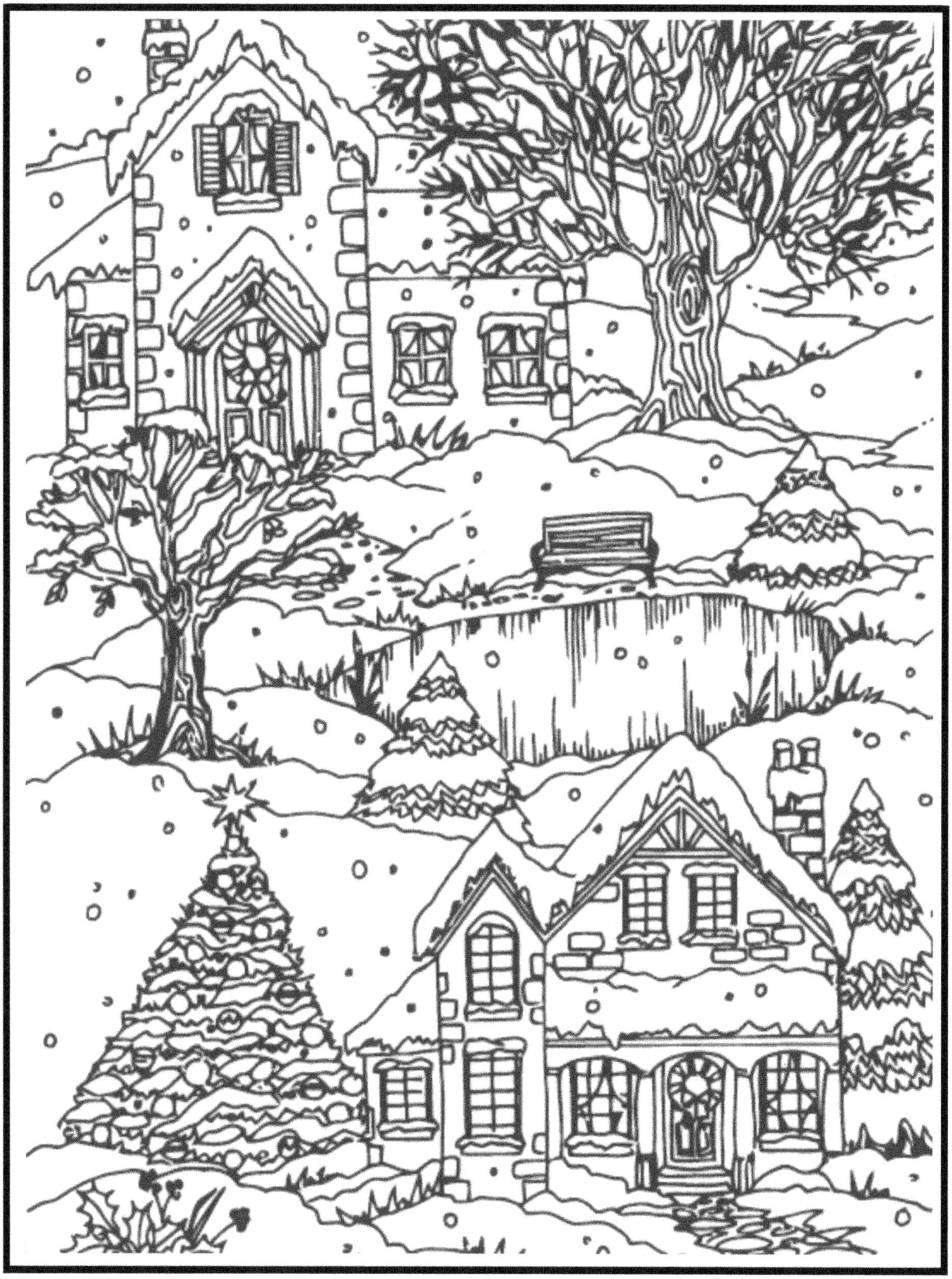

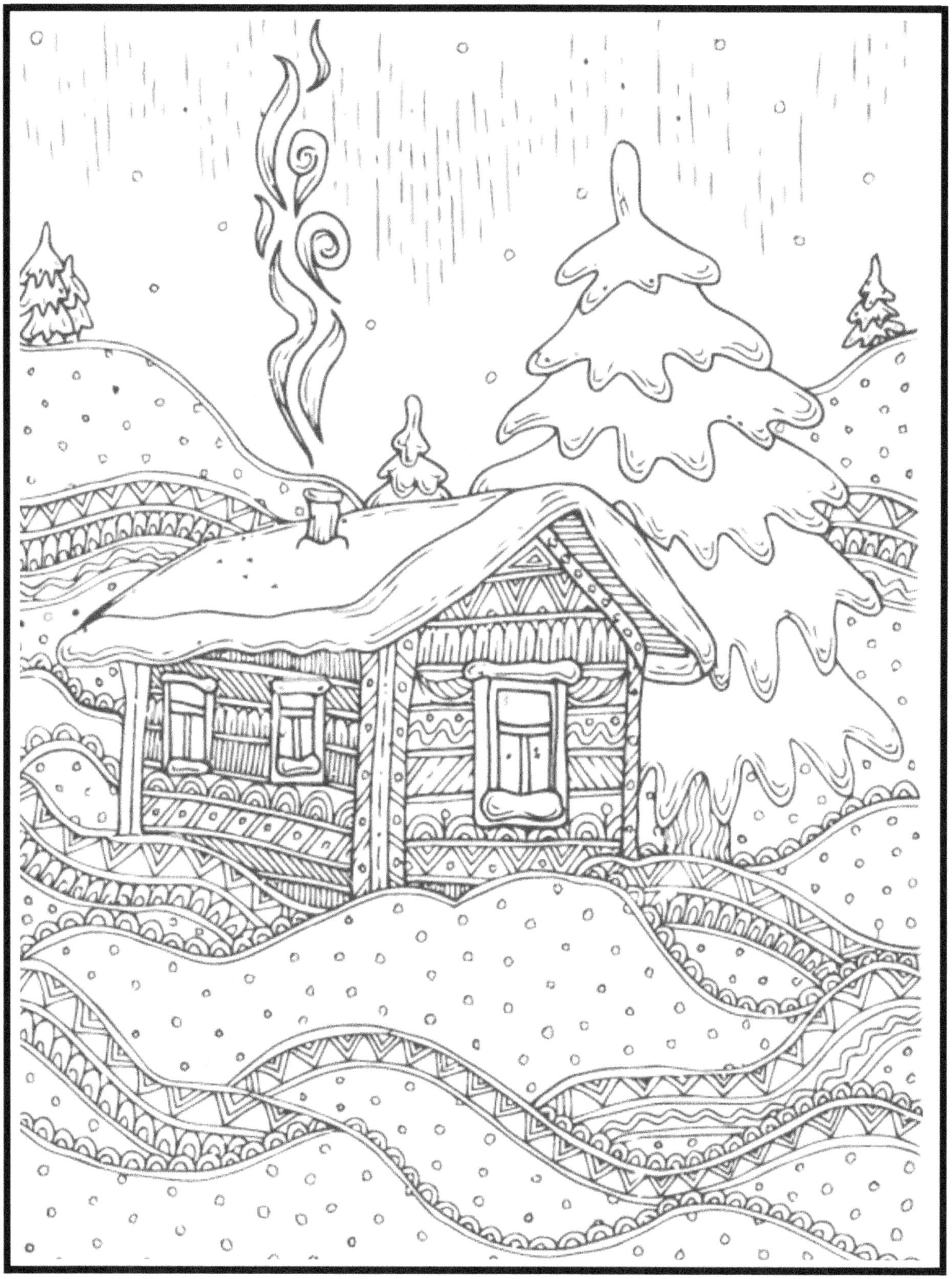

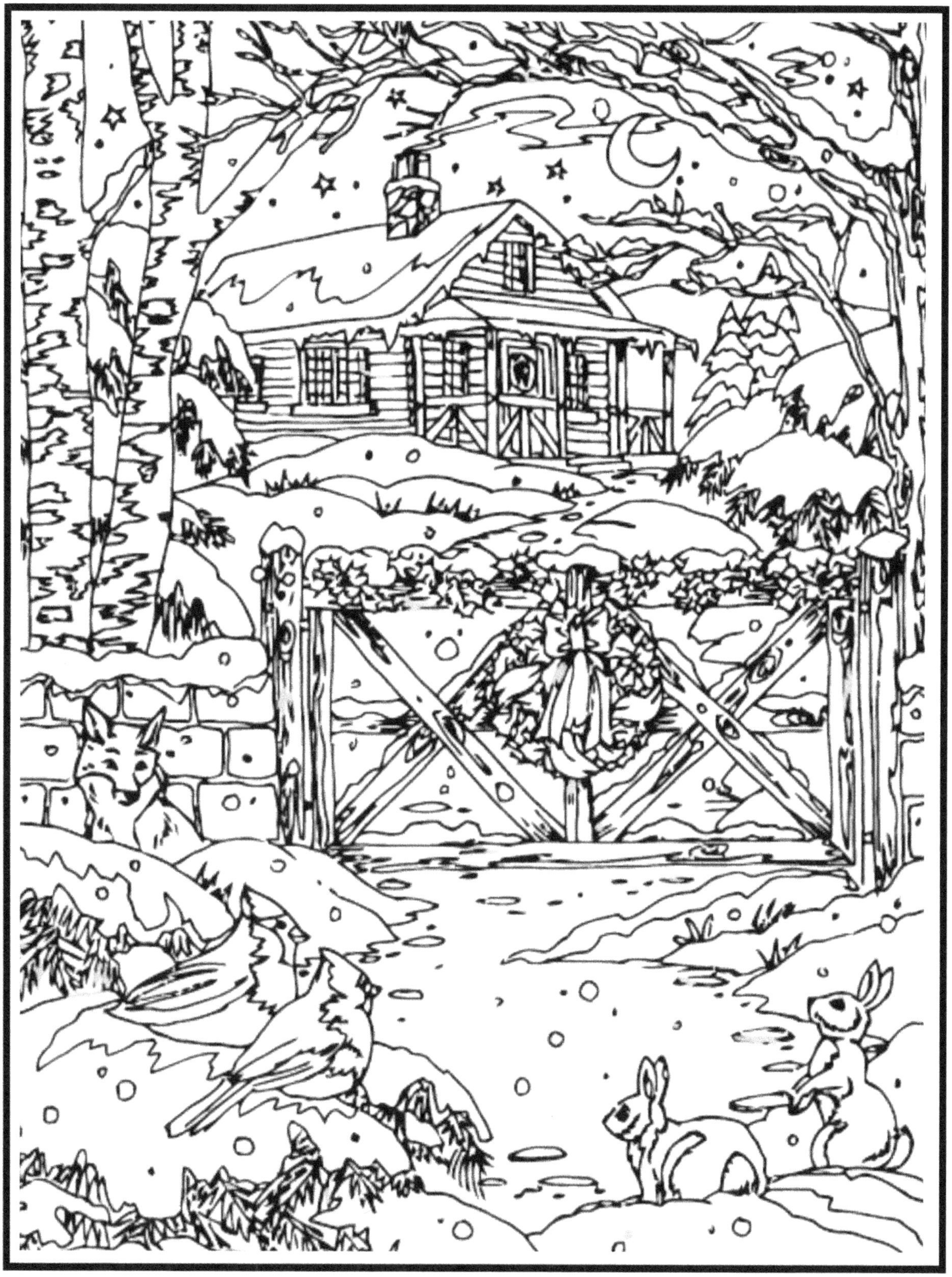

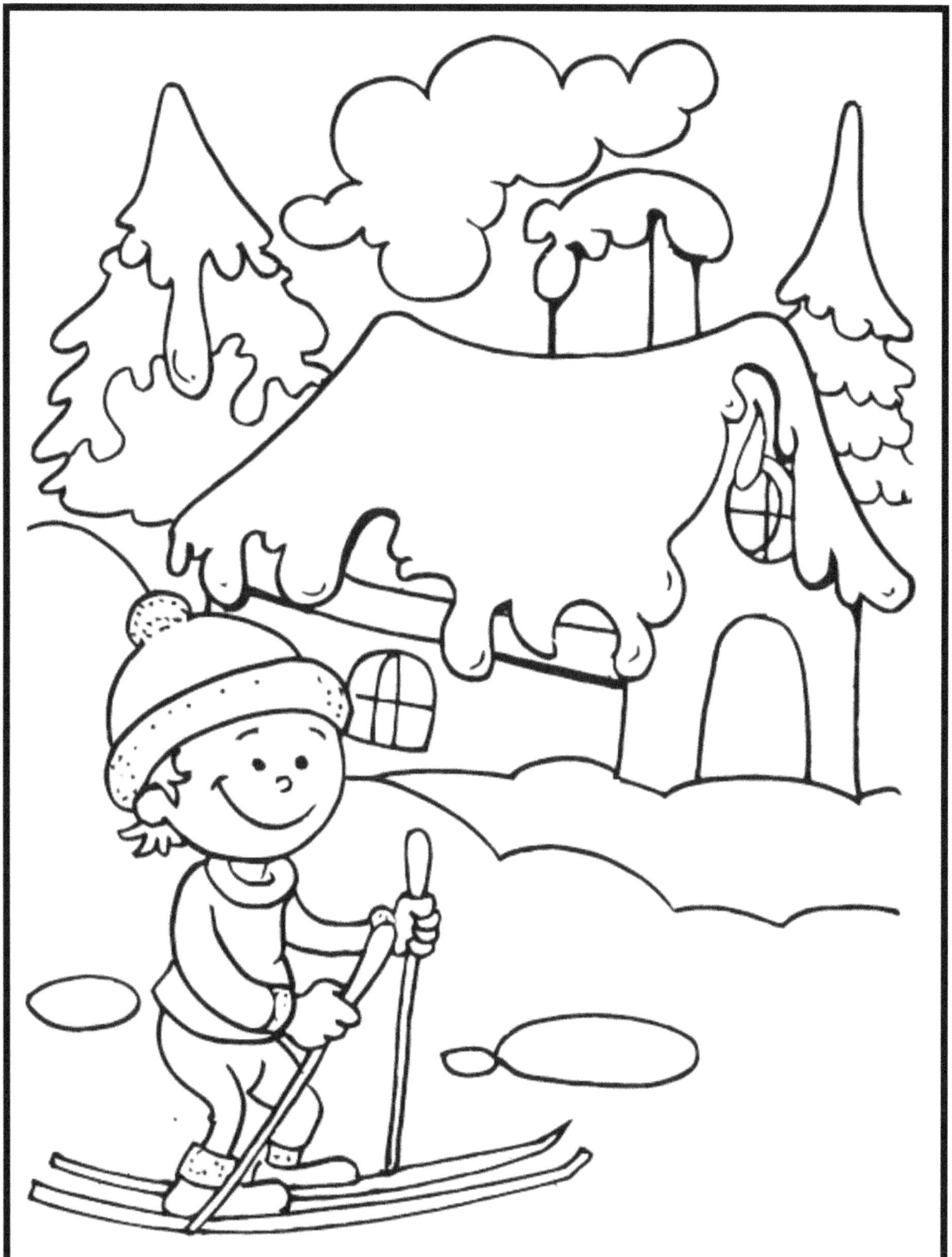

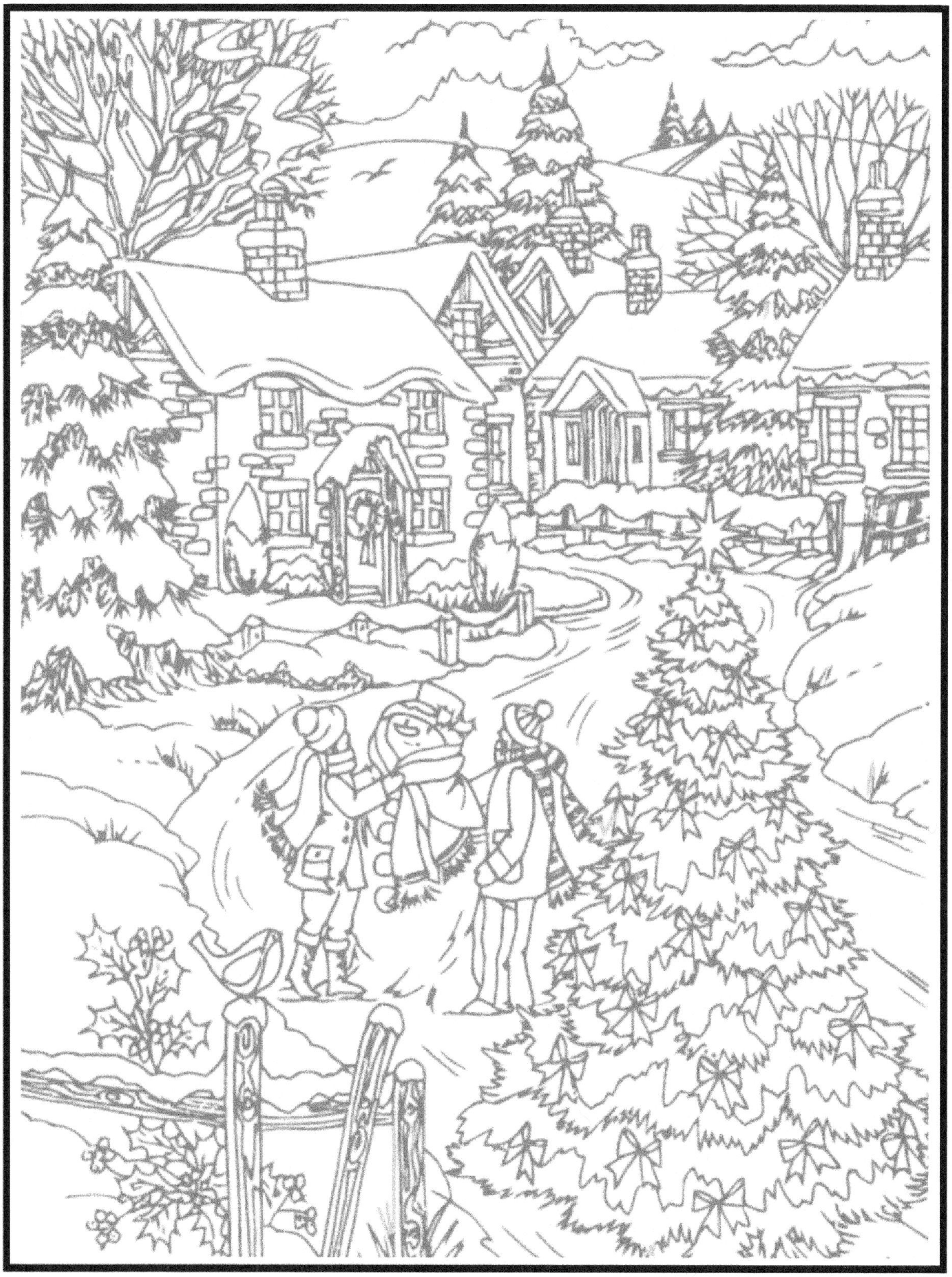

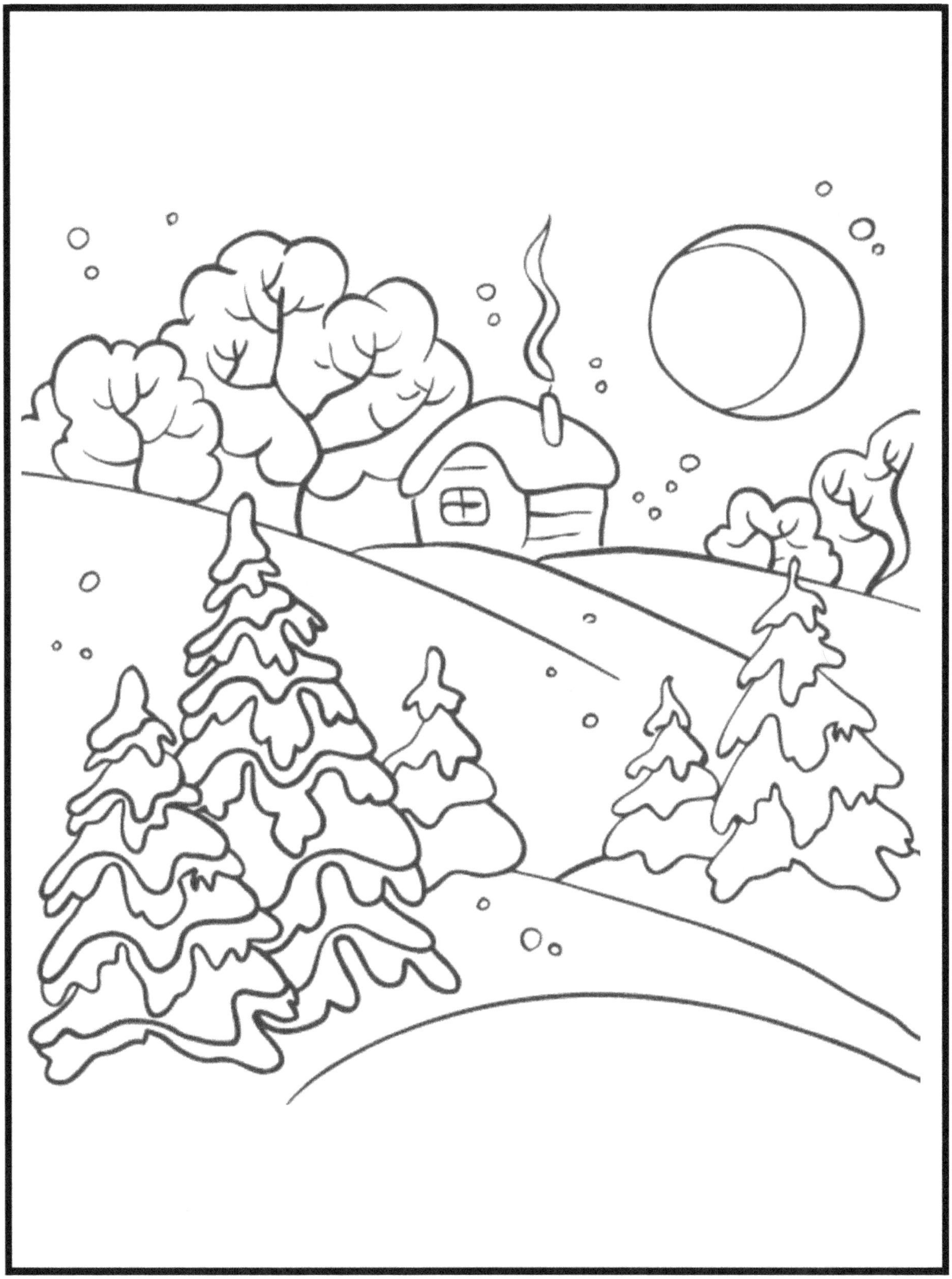

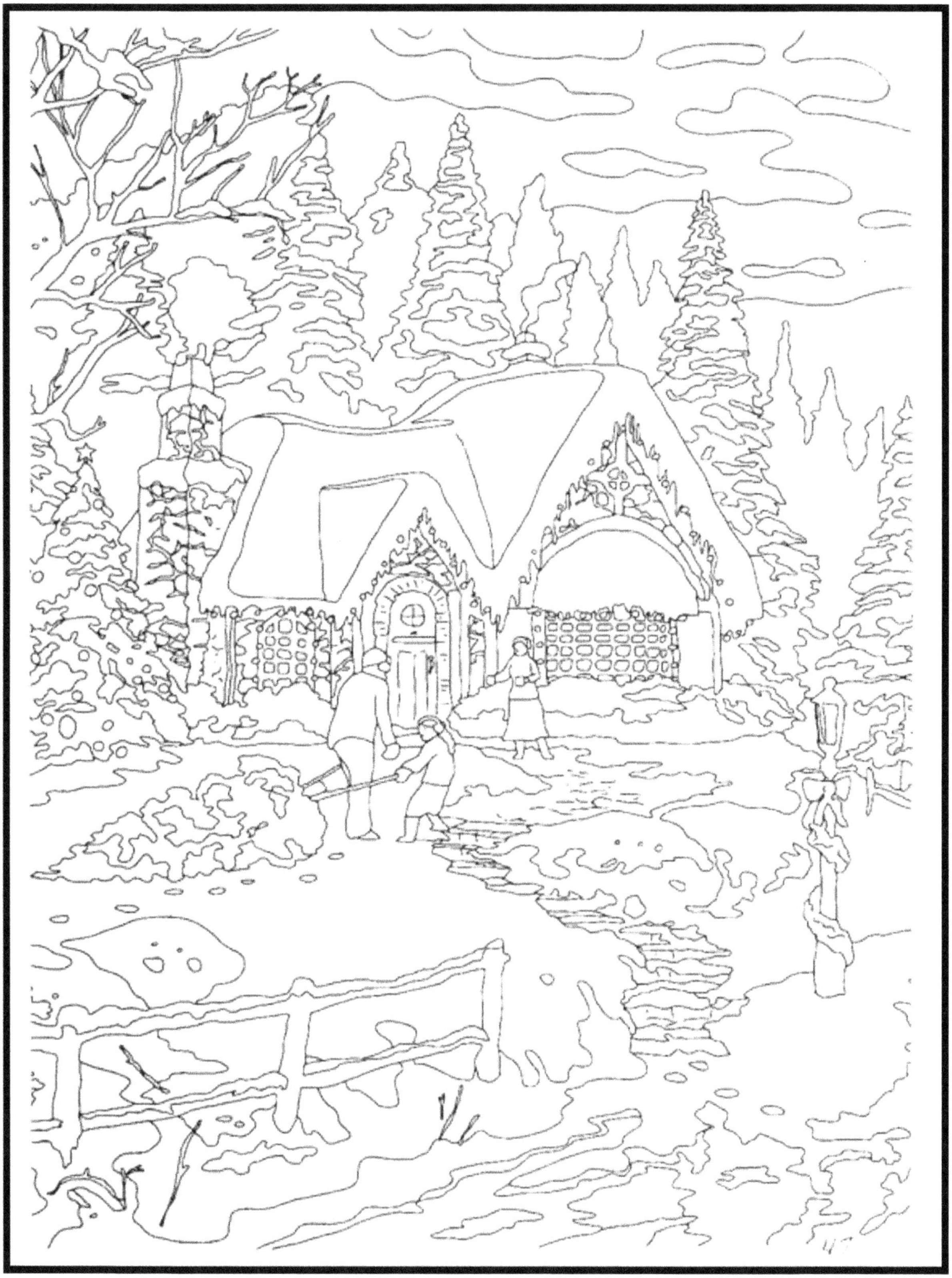

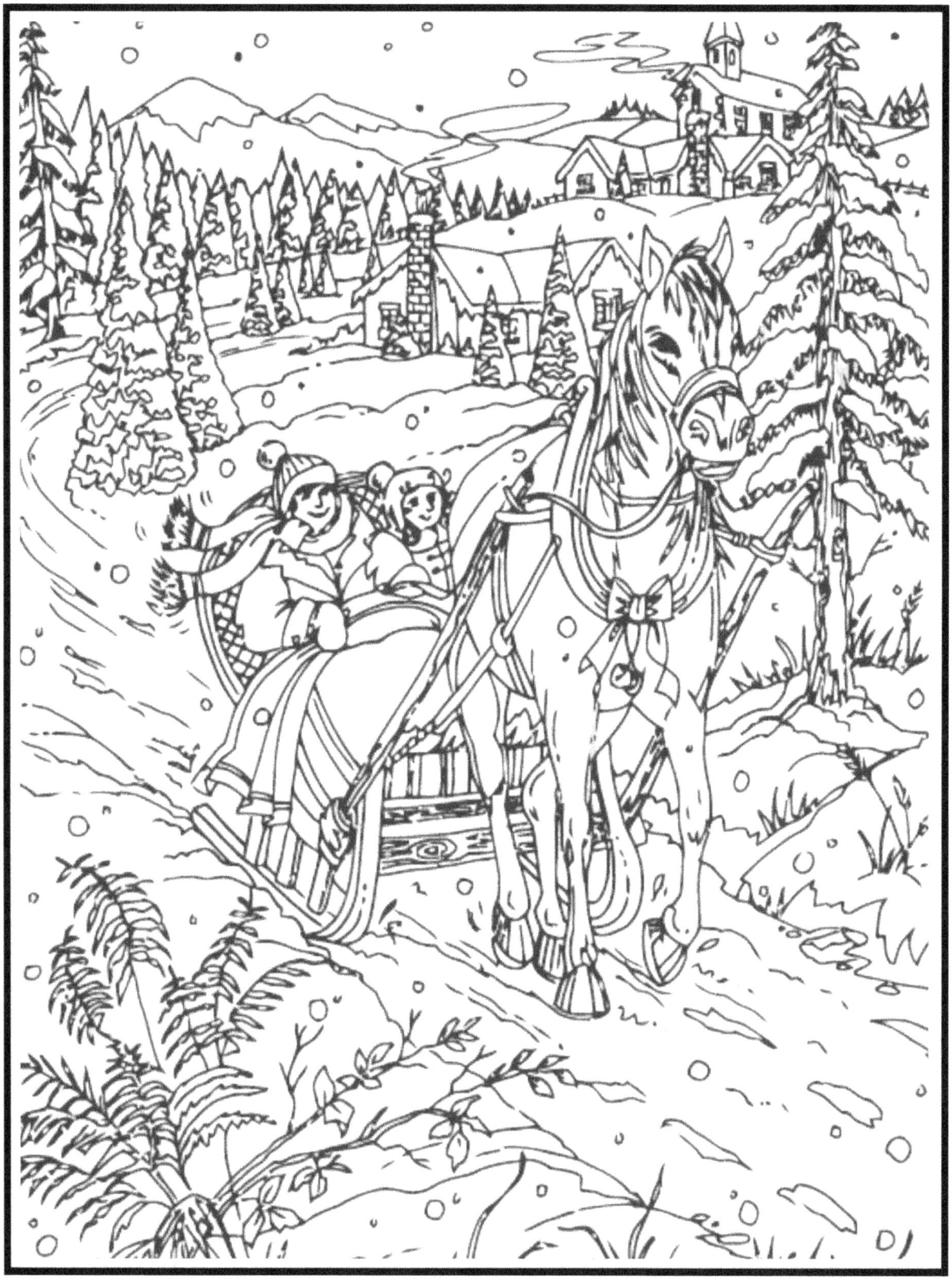

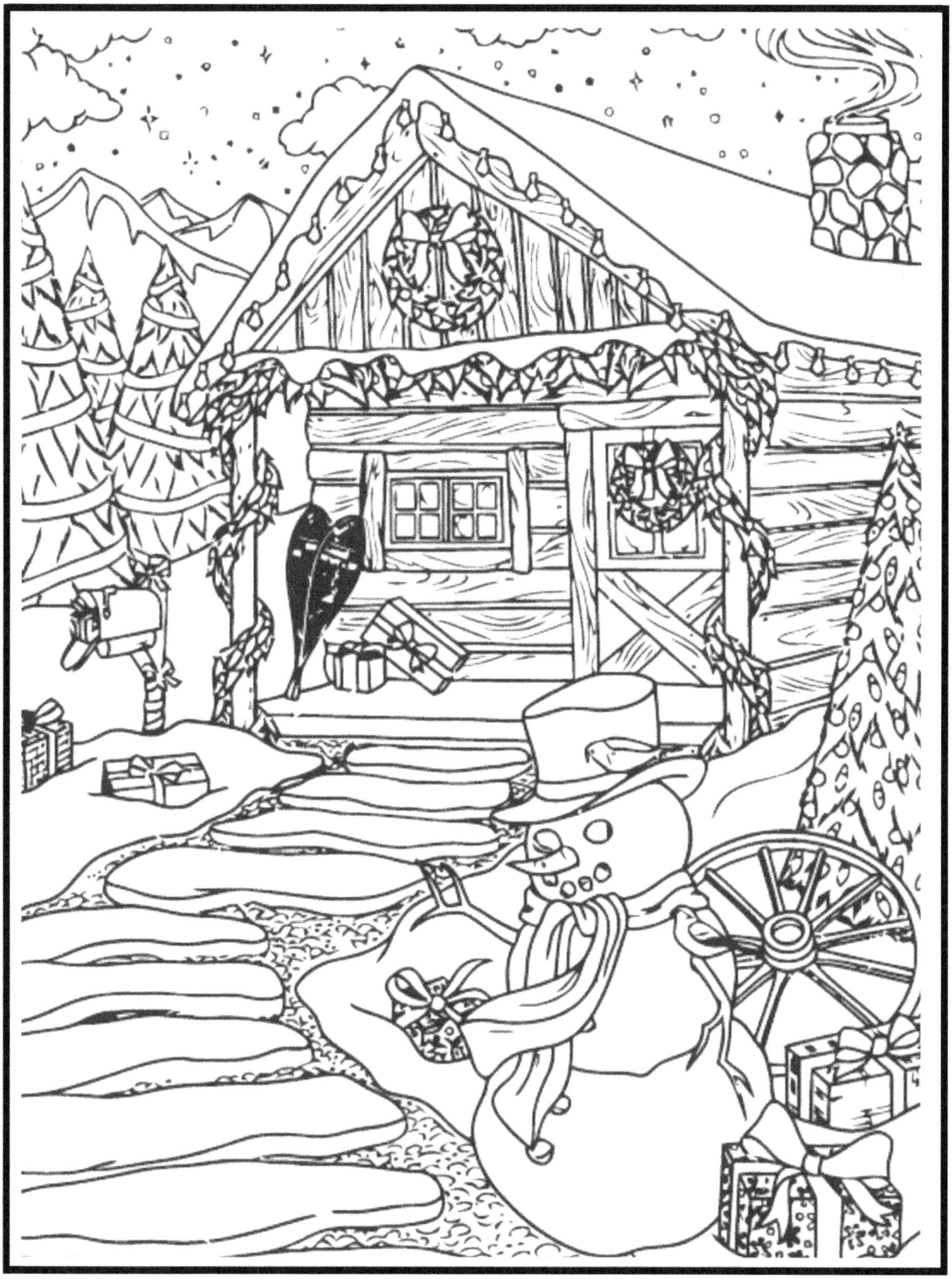

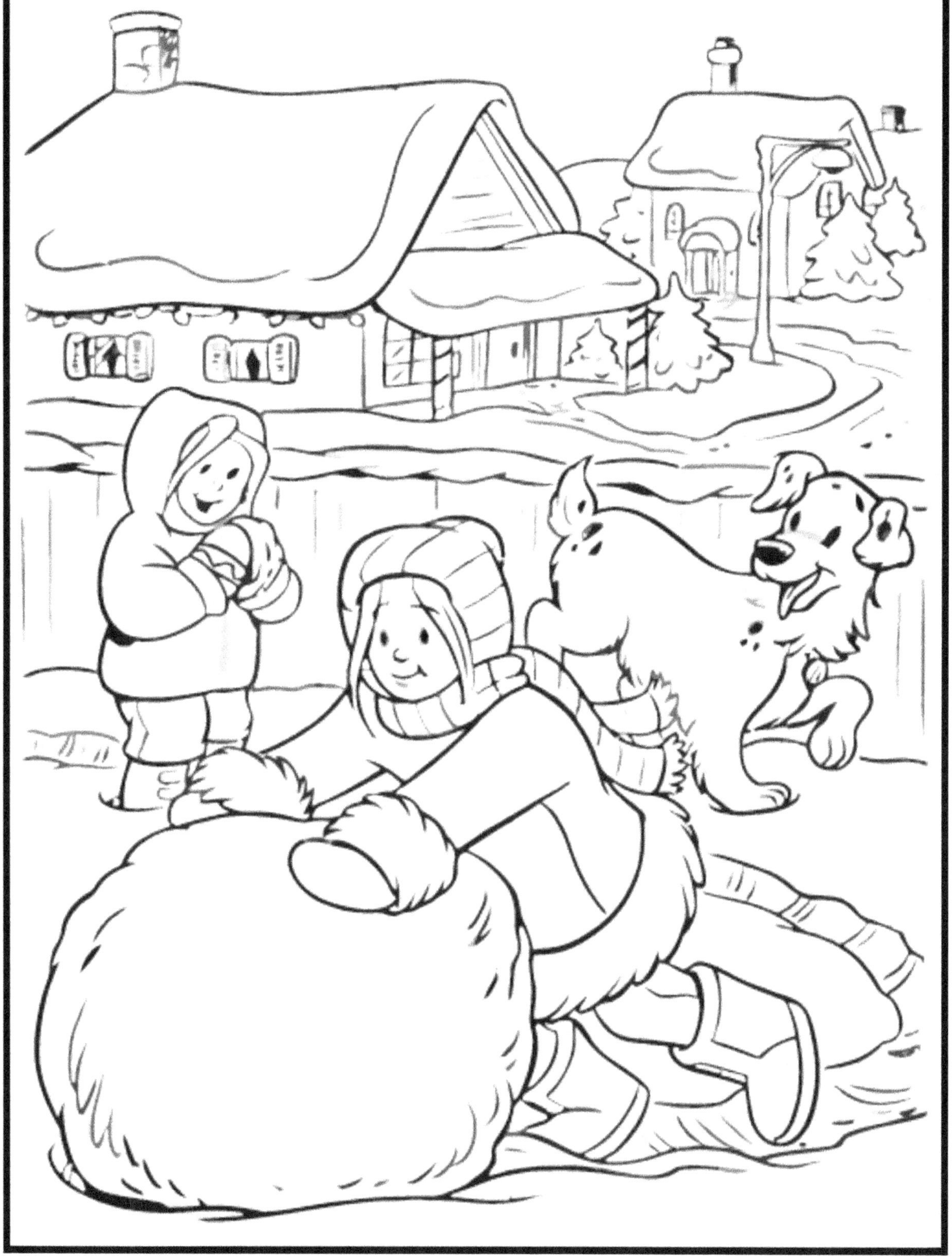

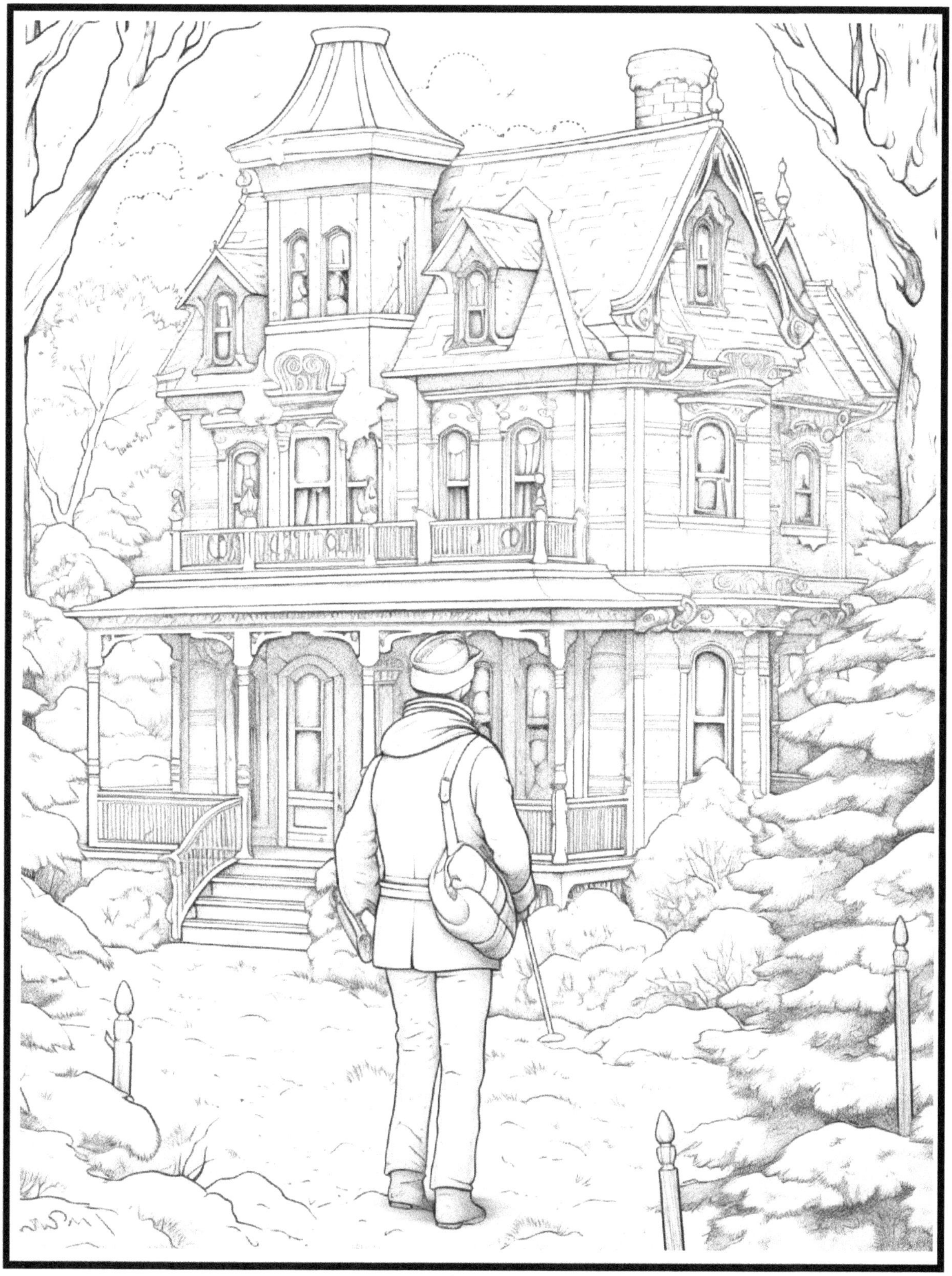

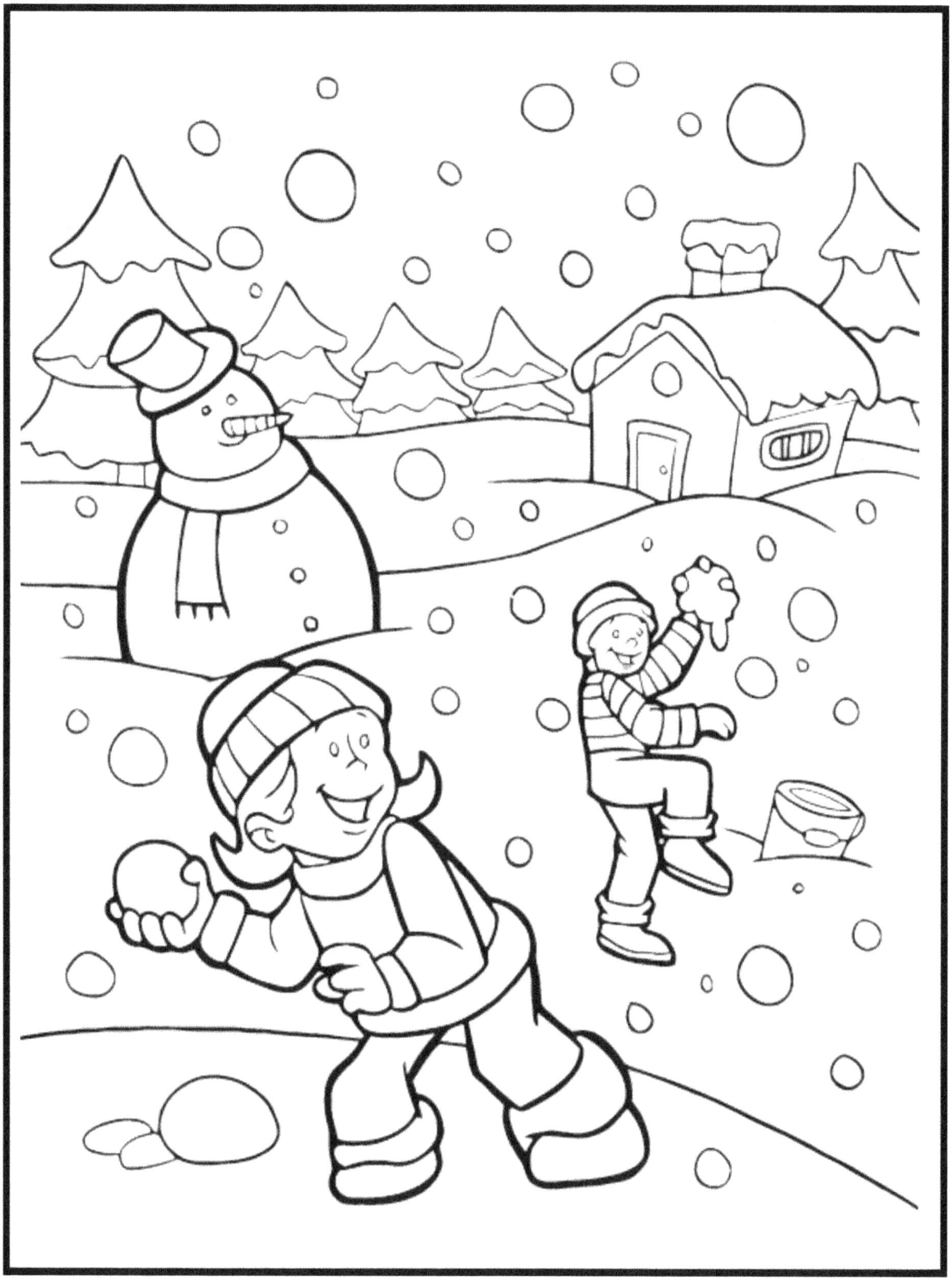

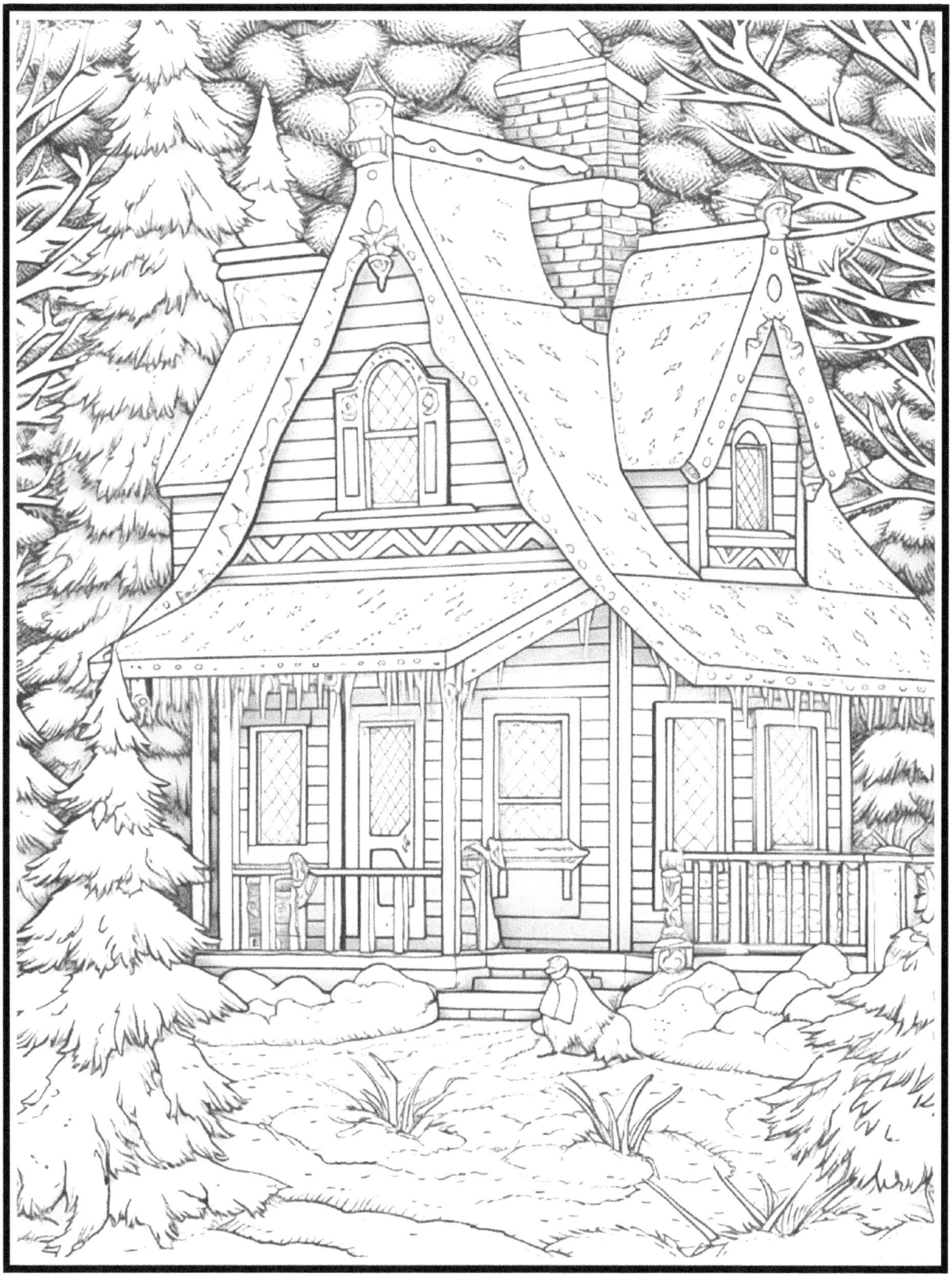

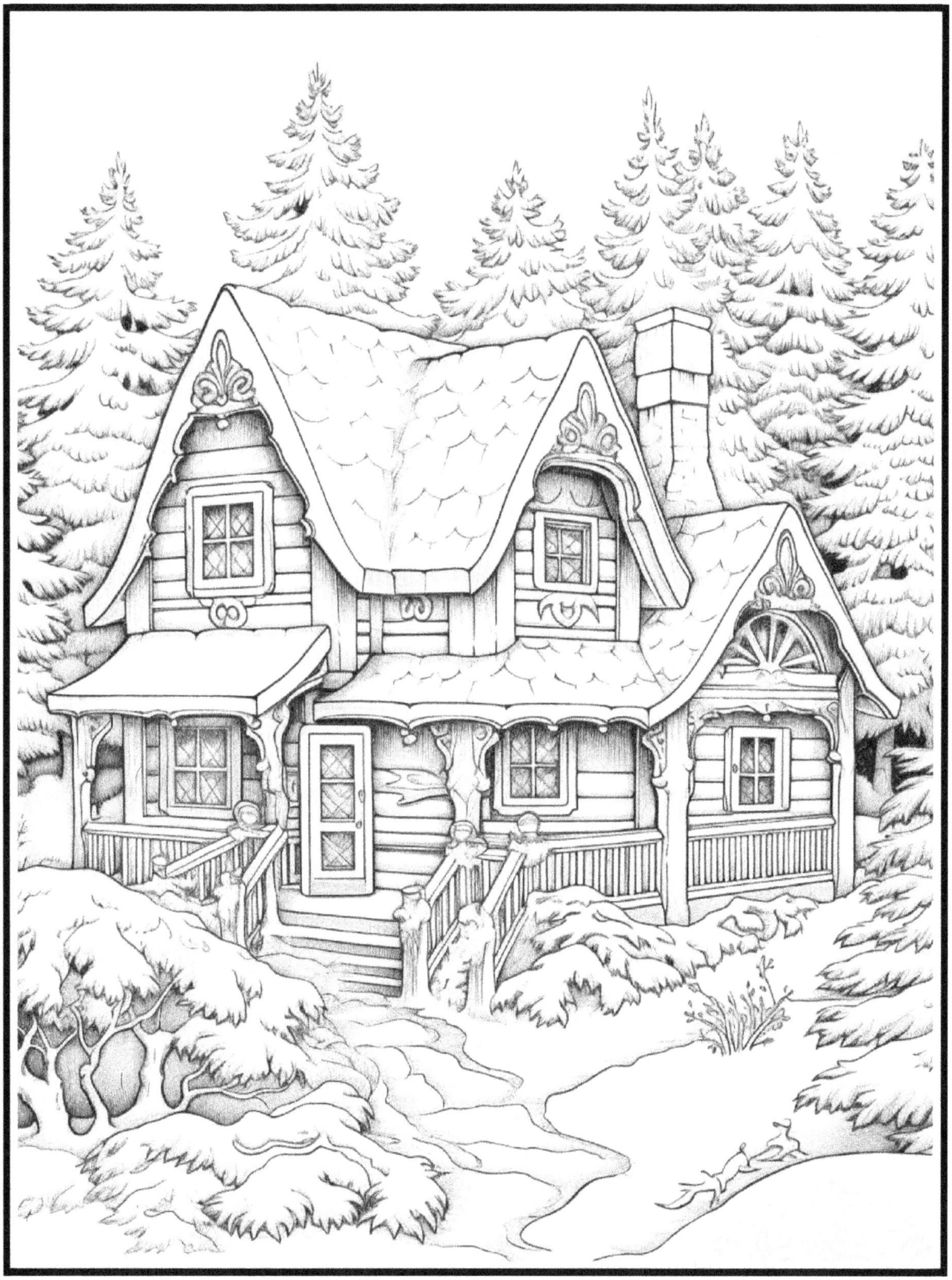

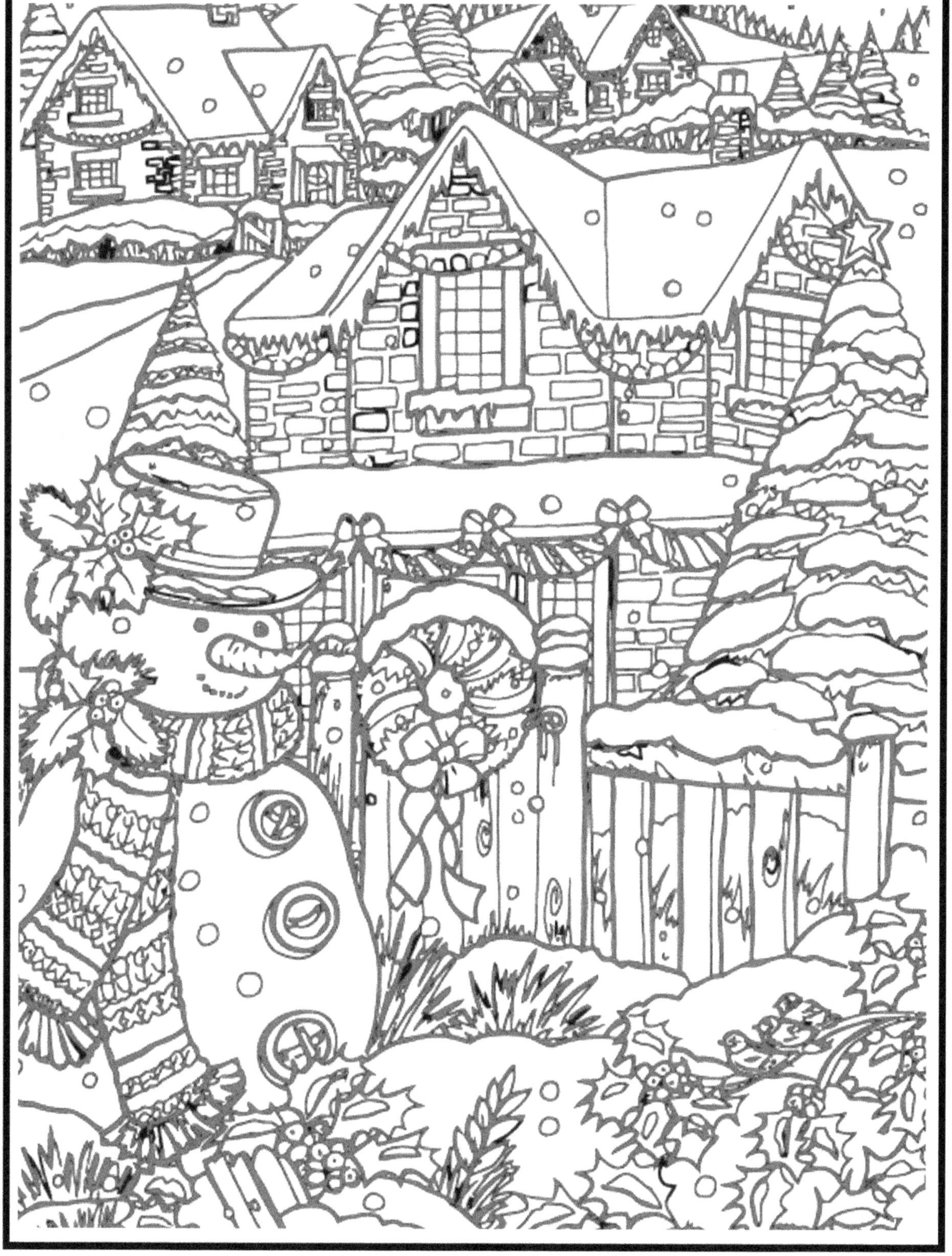

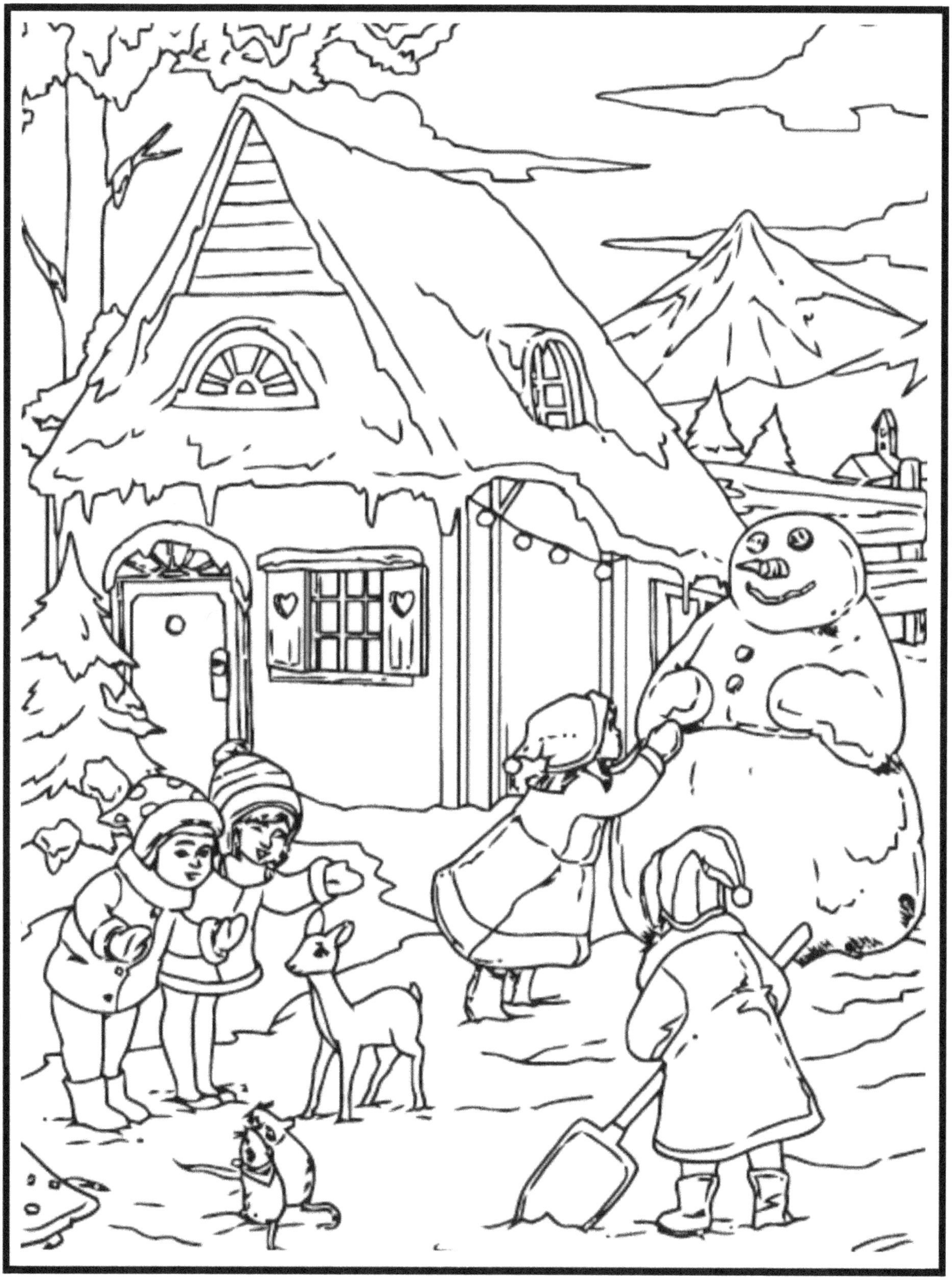

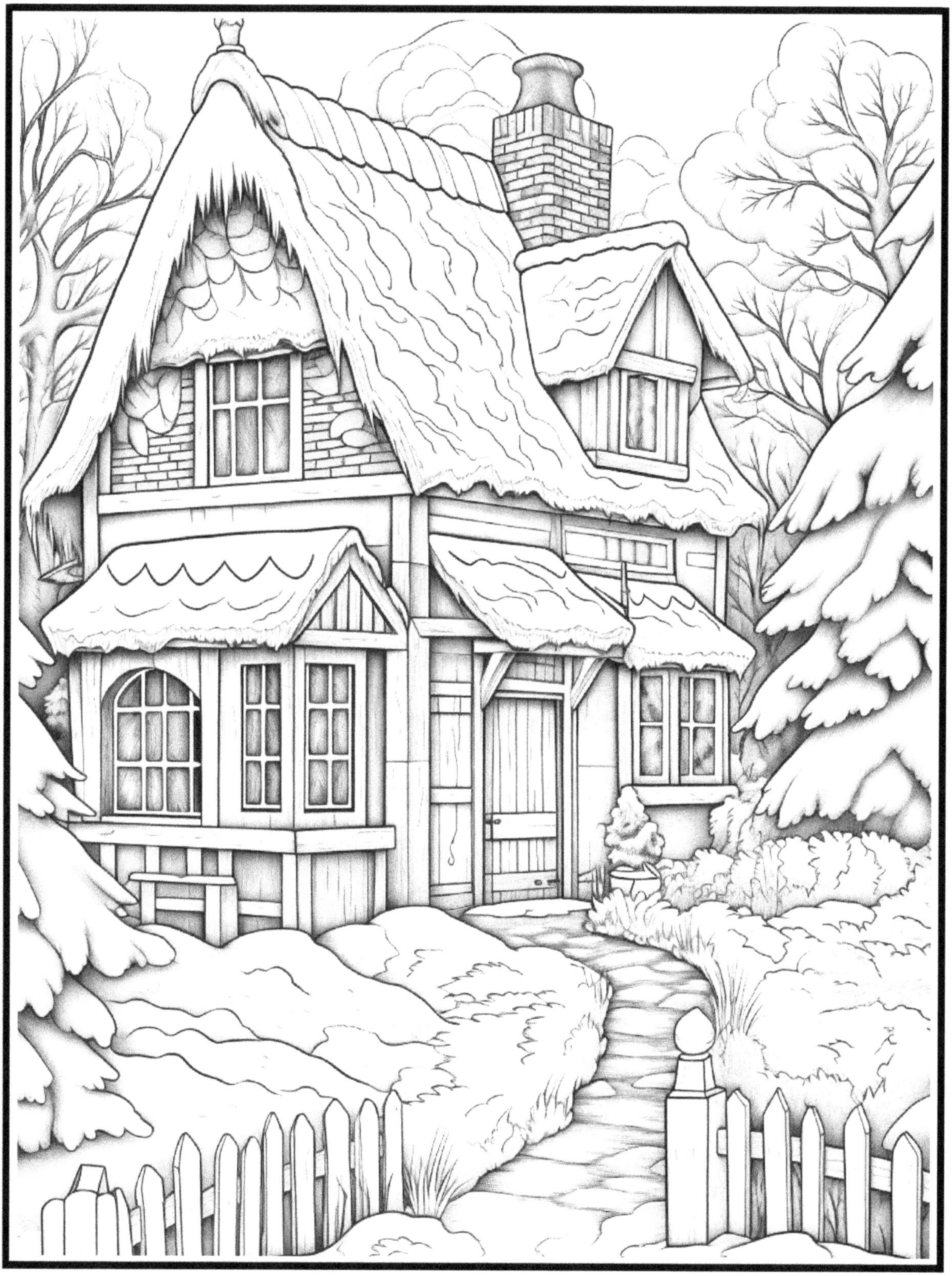

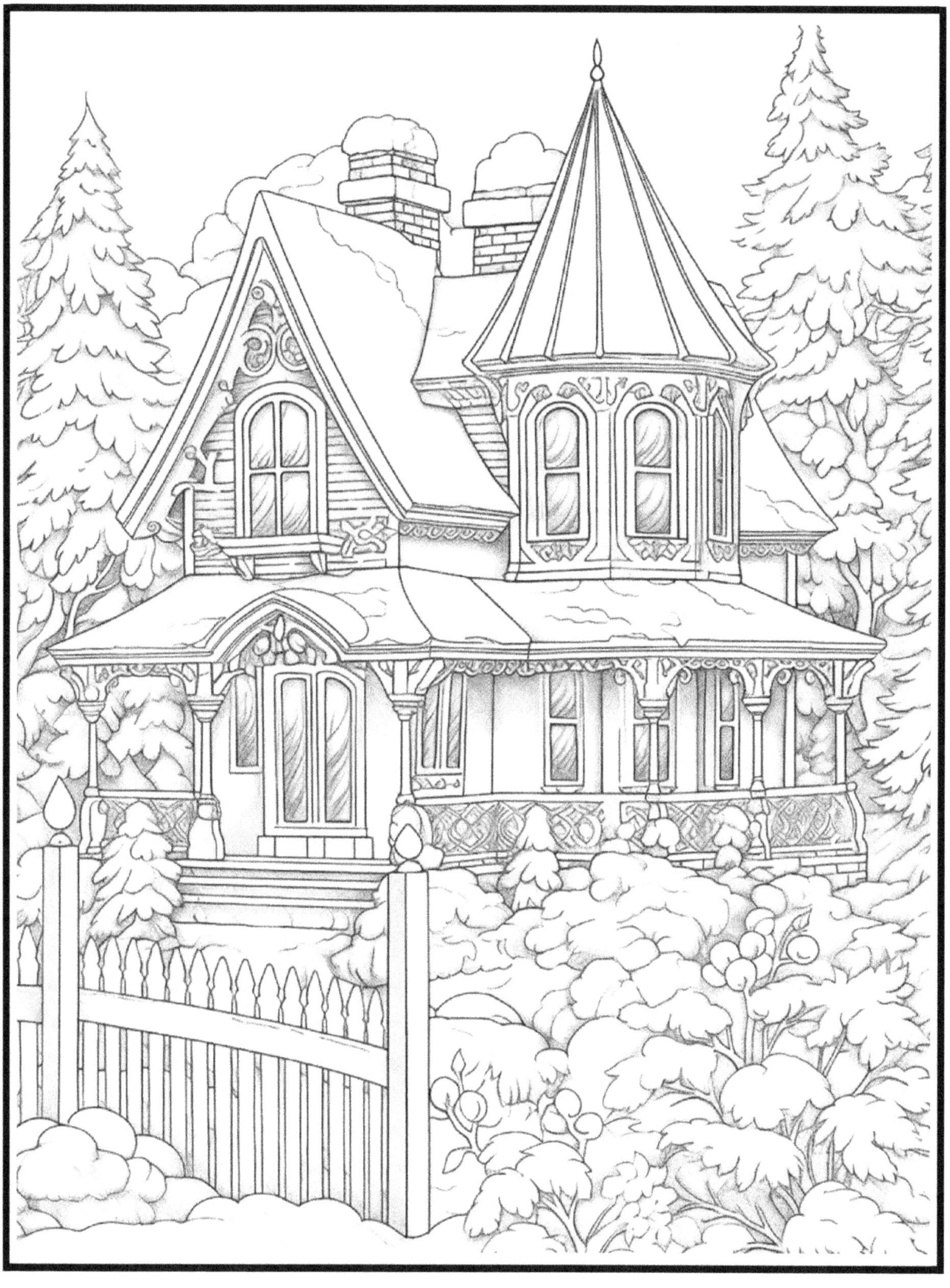

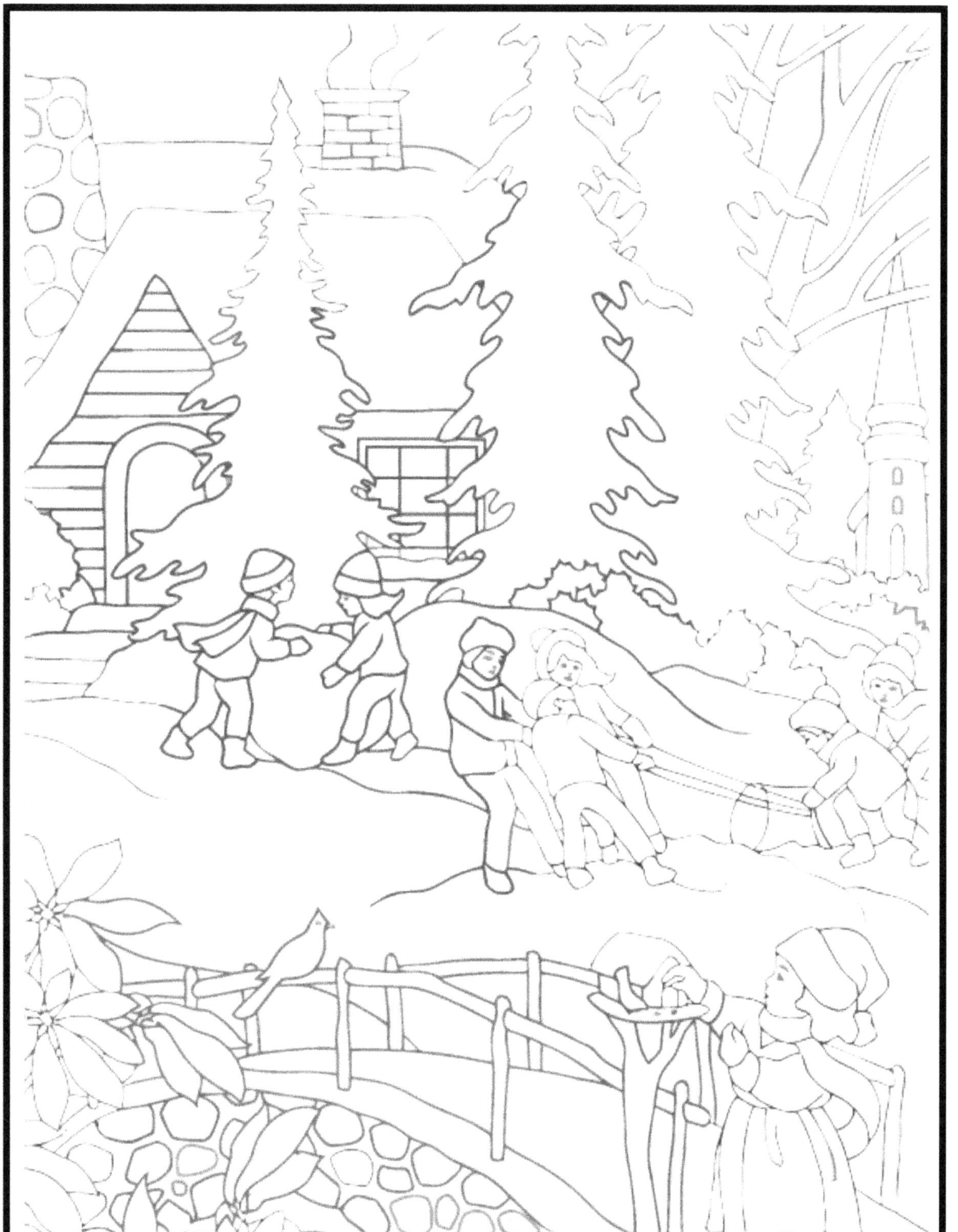

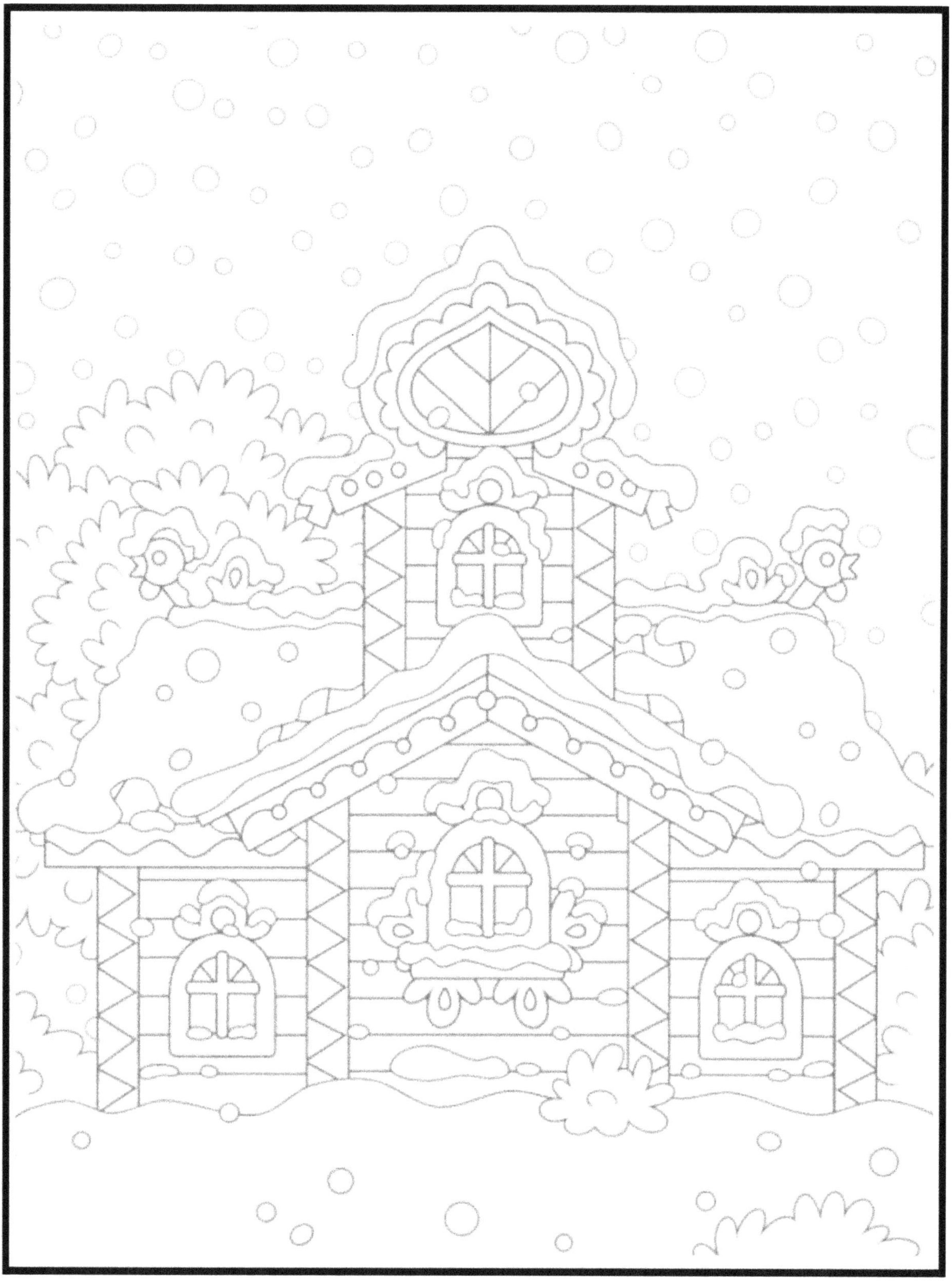

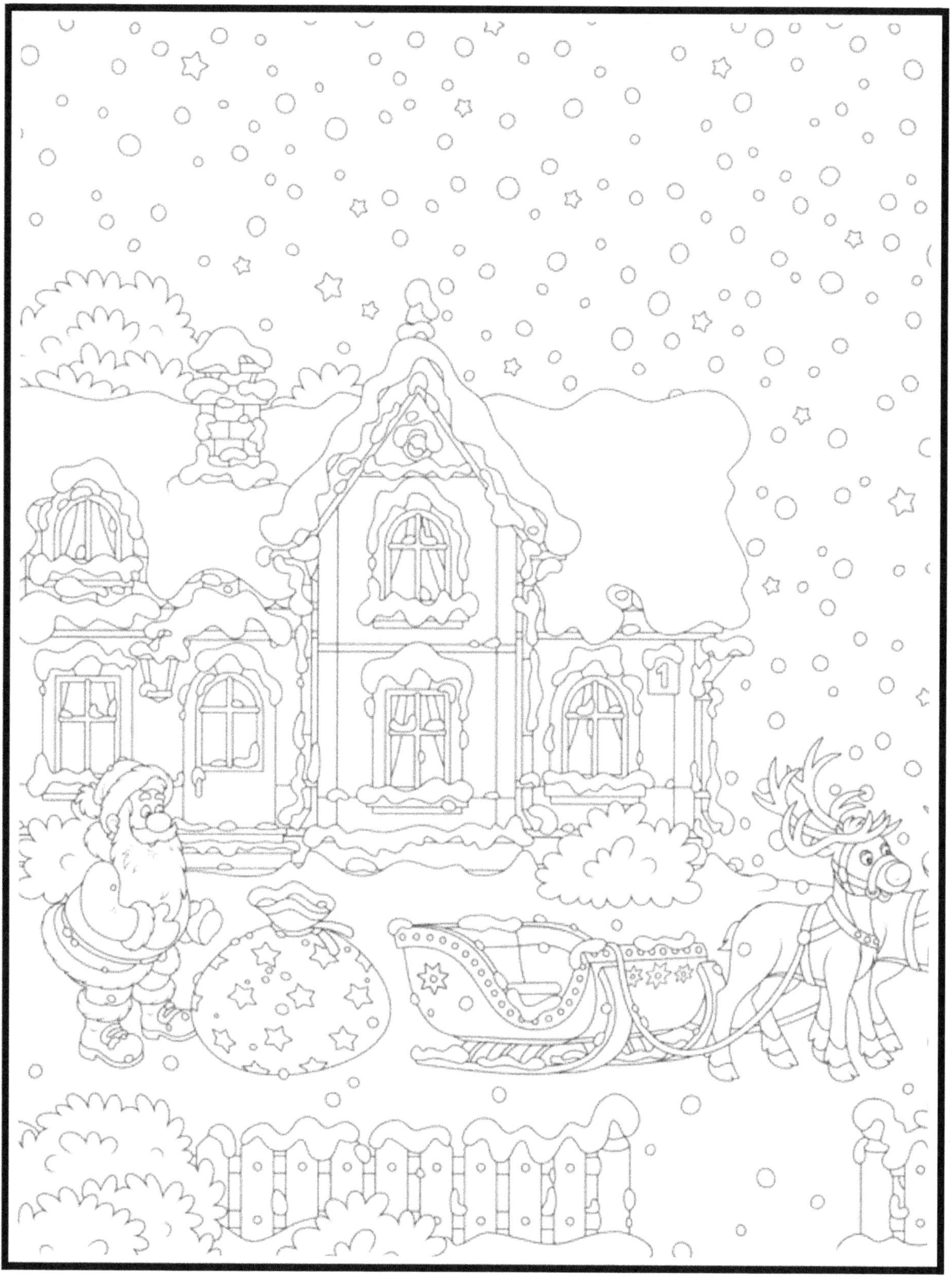
1

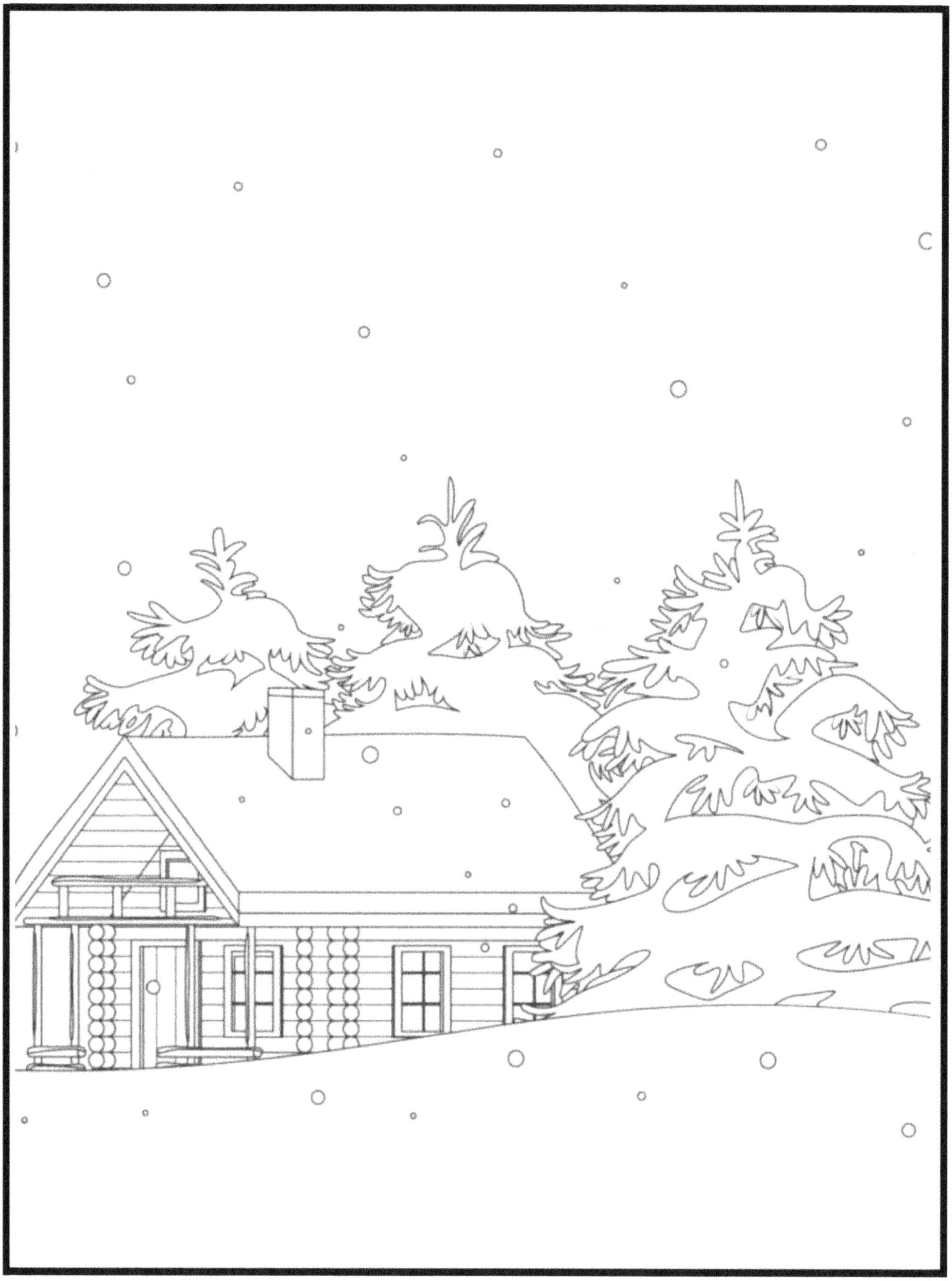

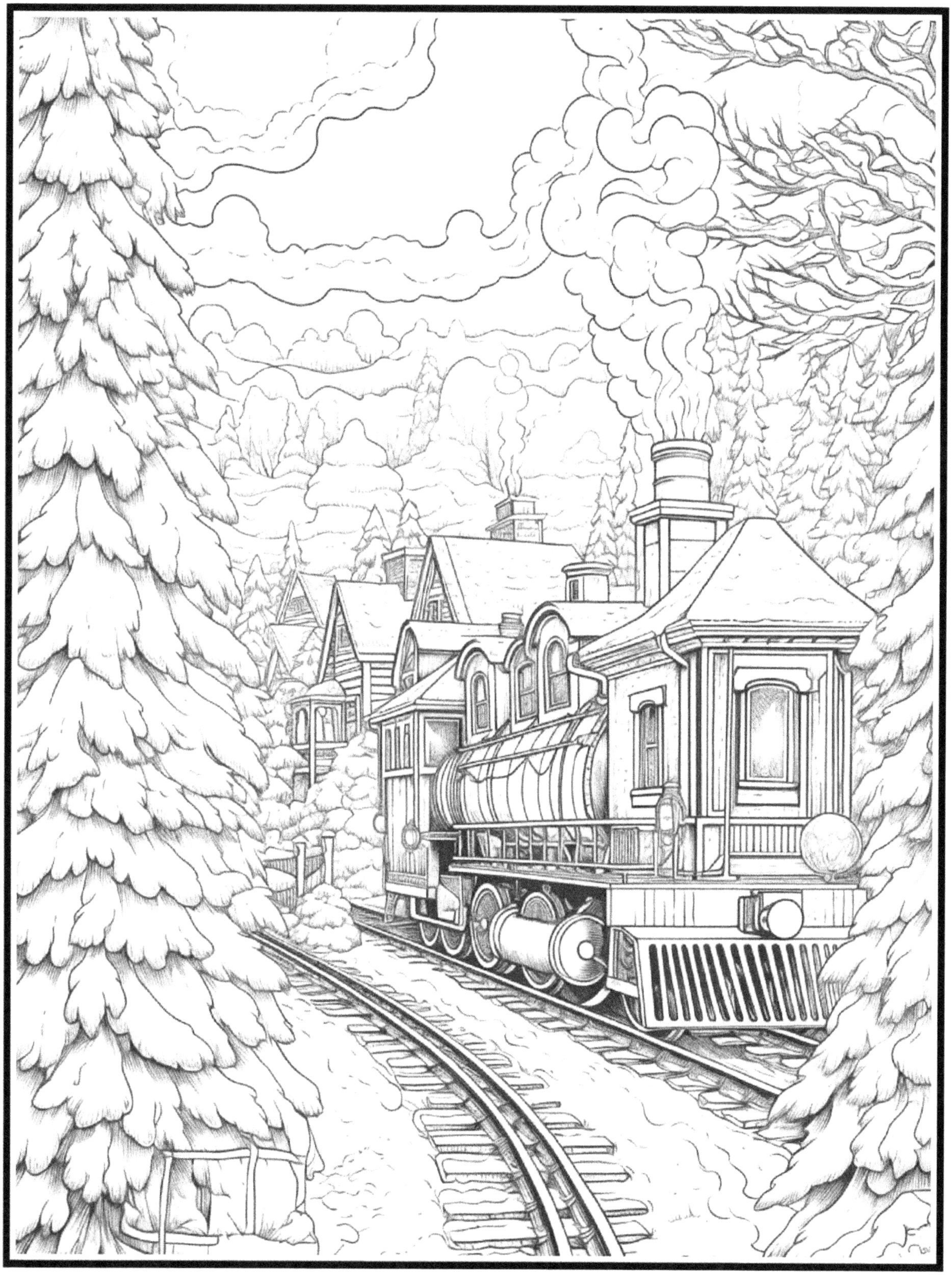

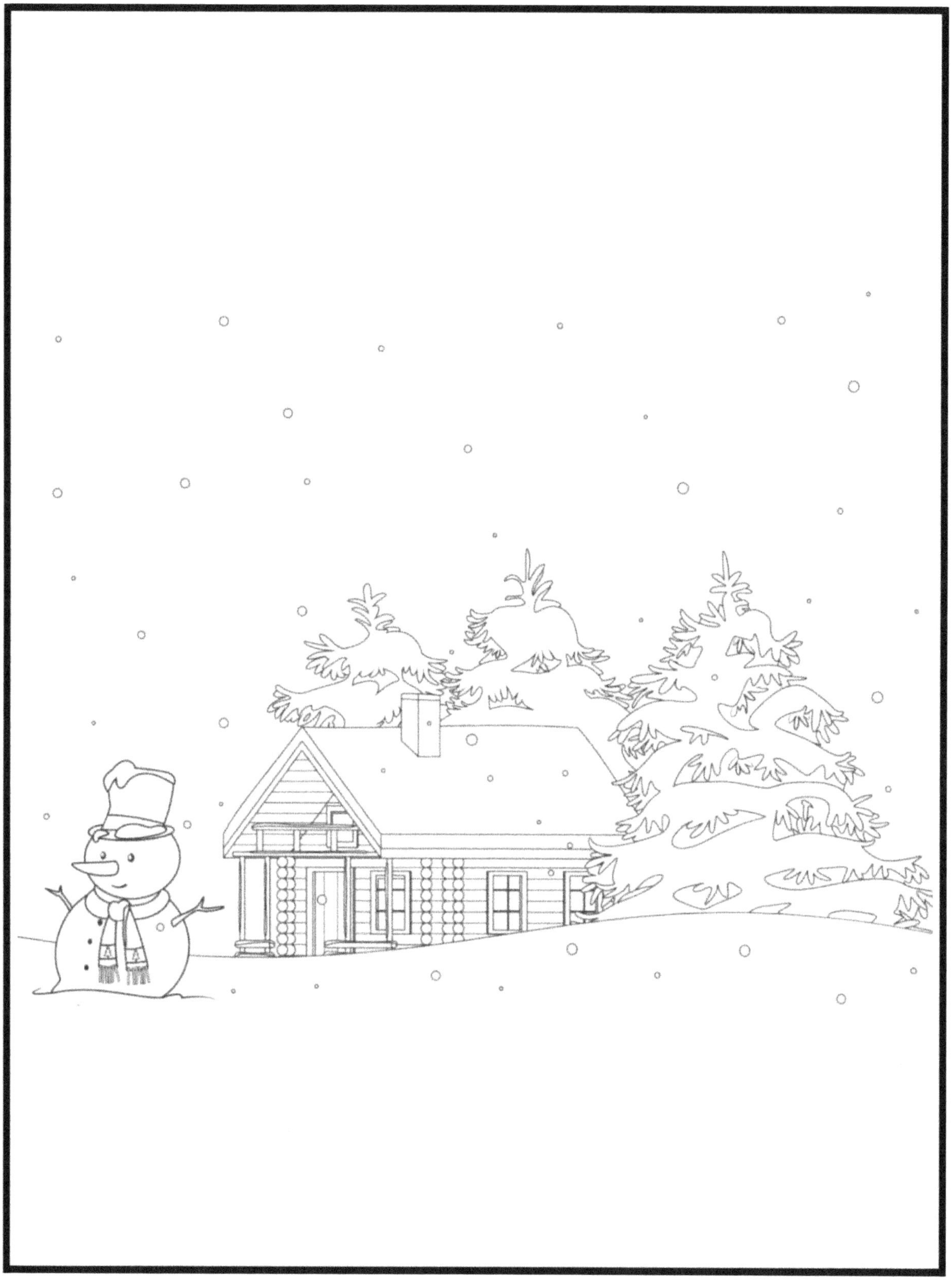

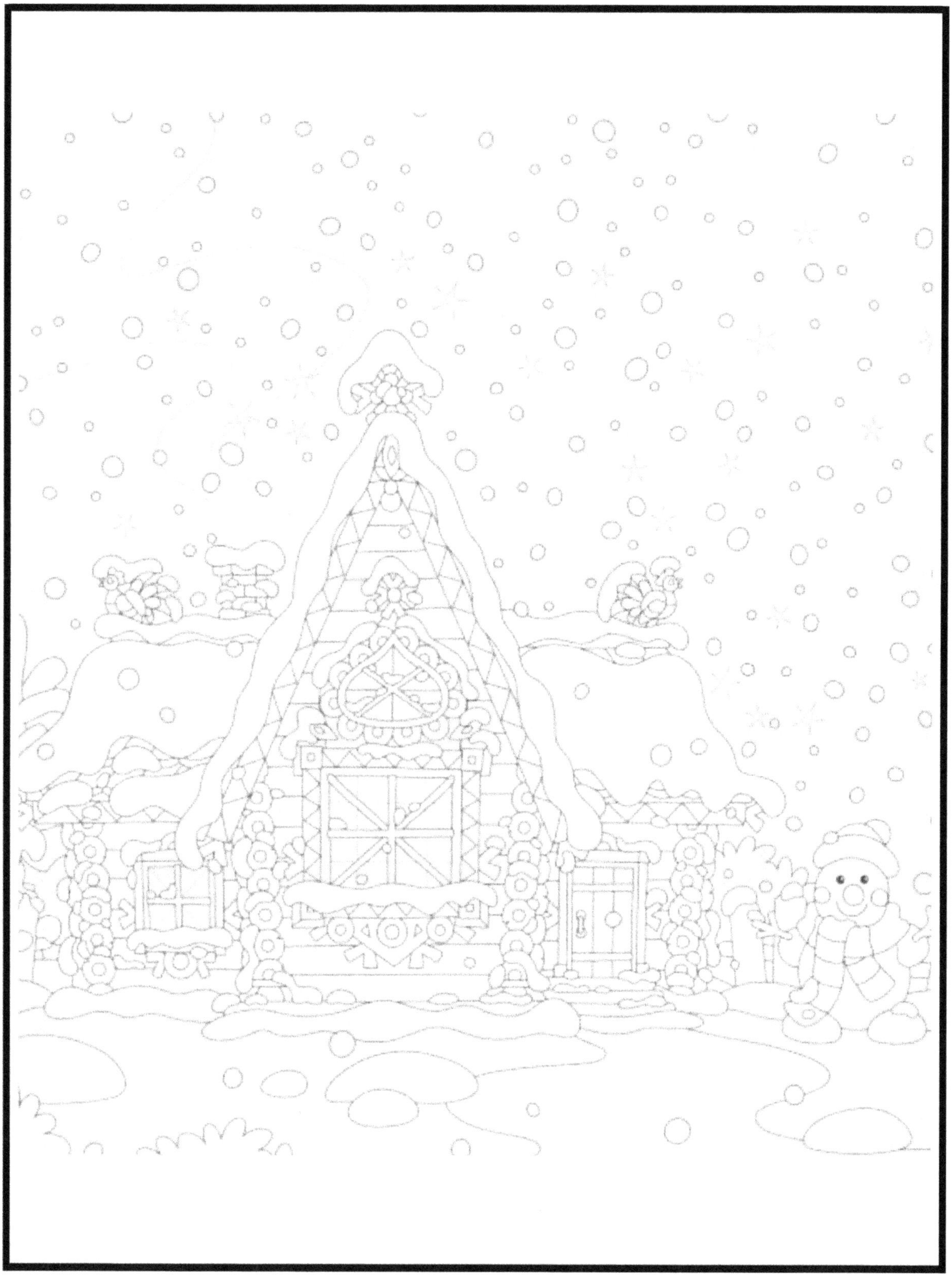

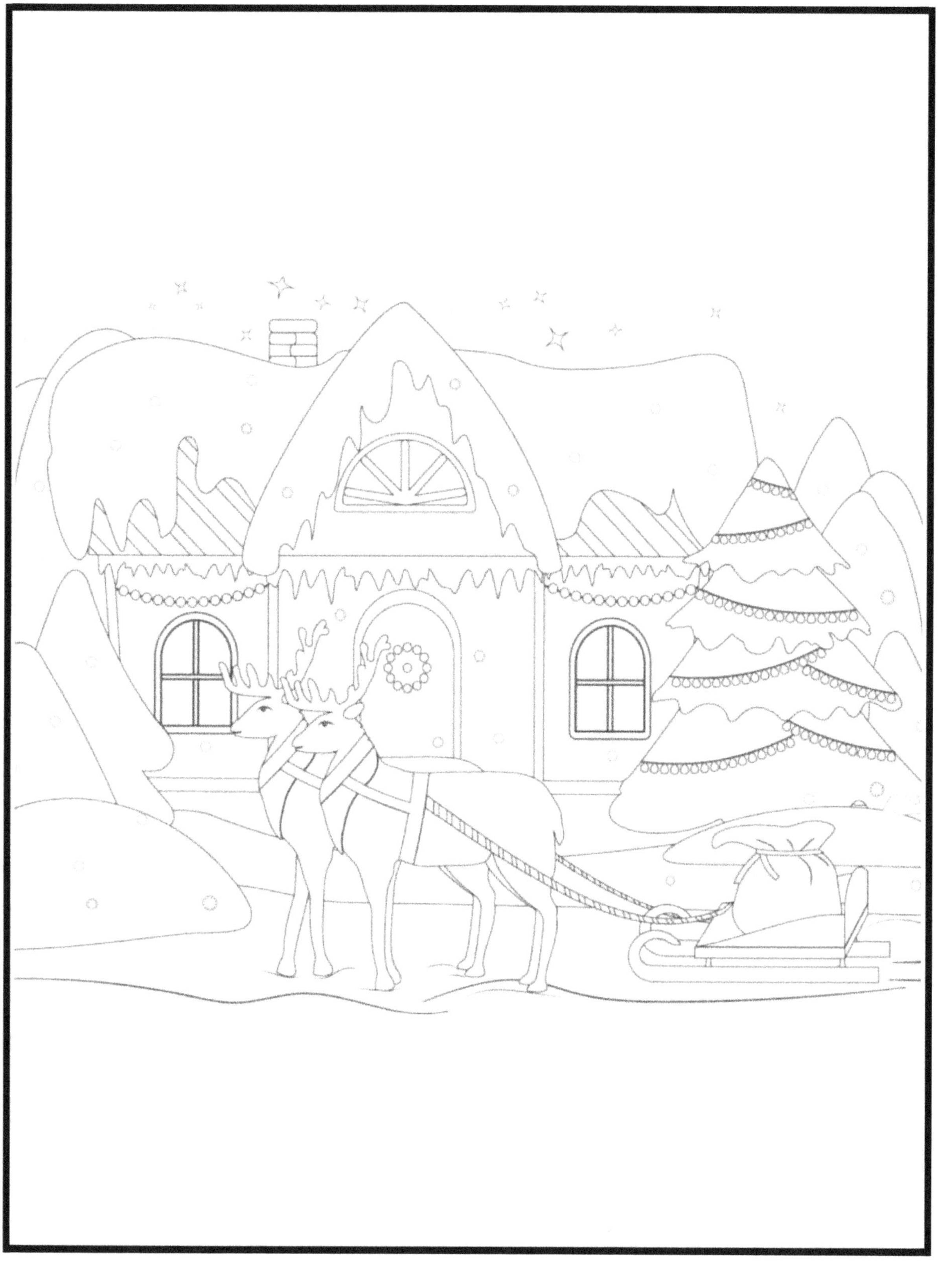

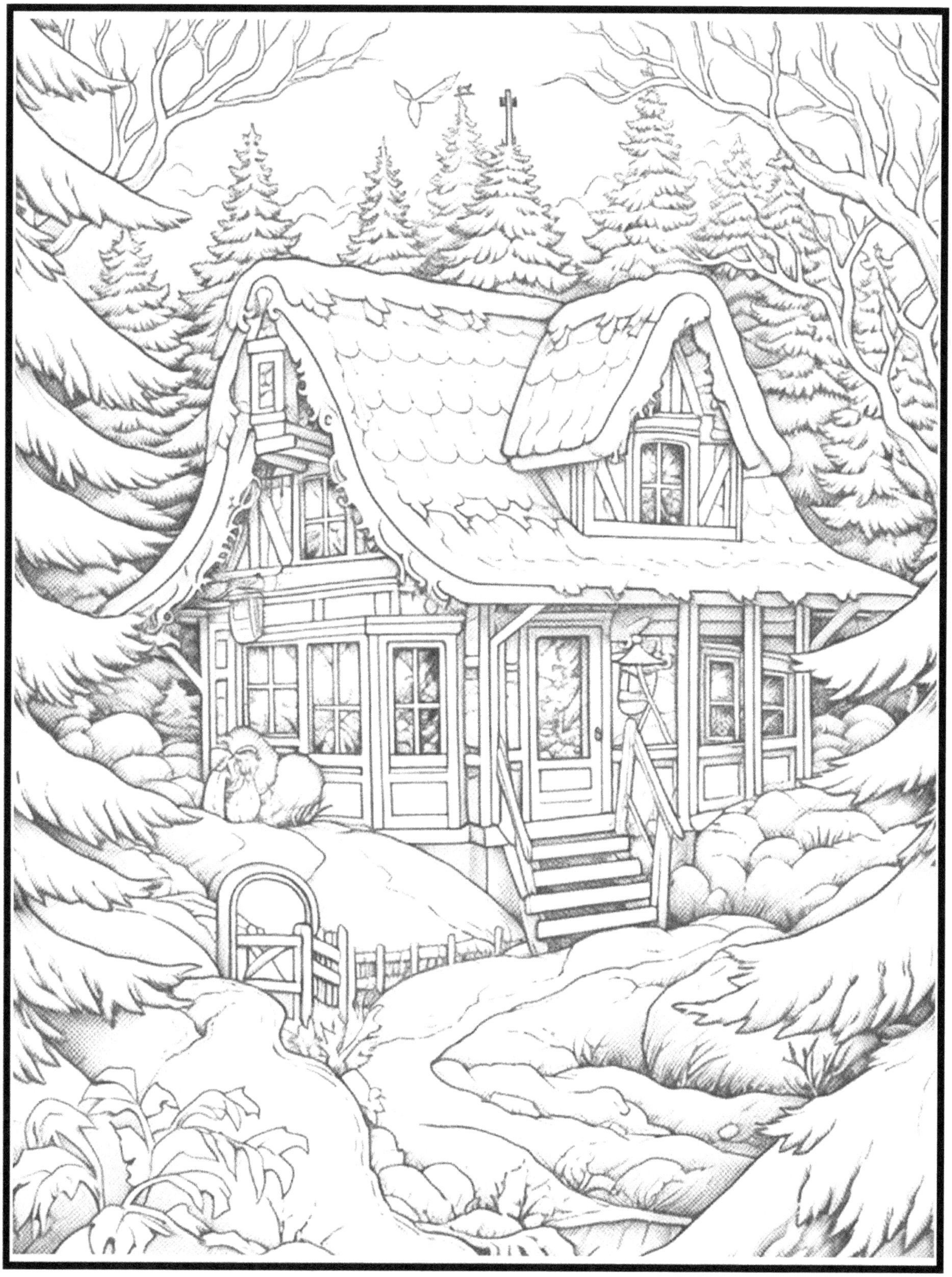

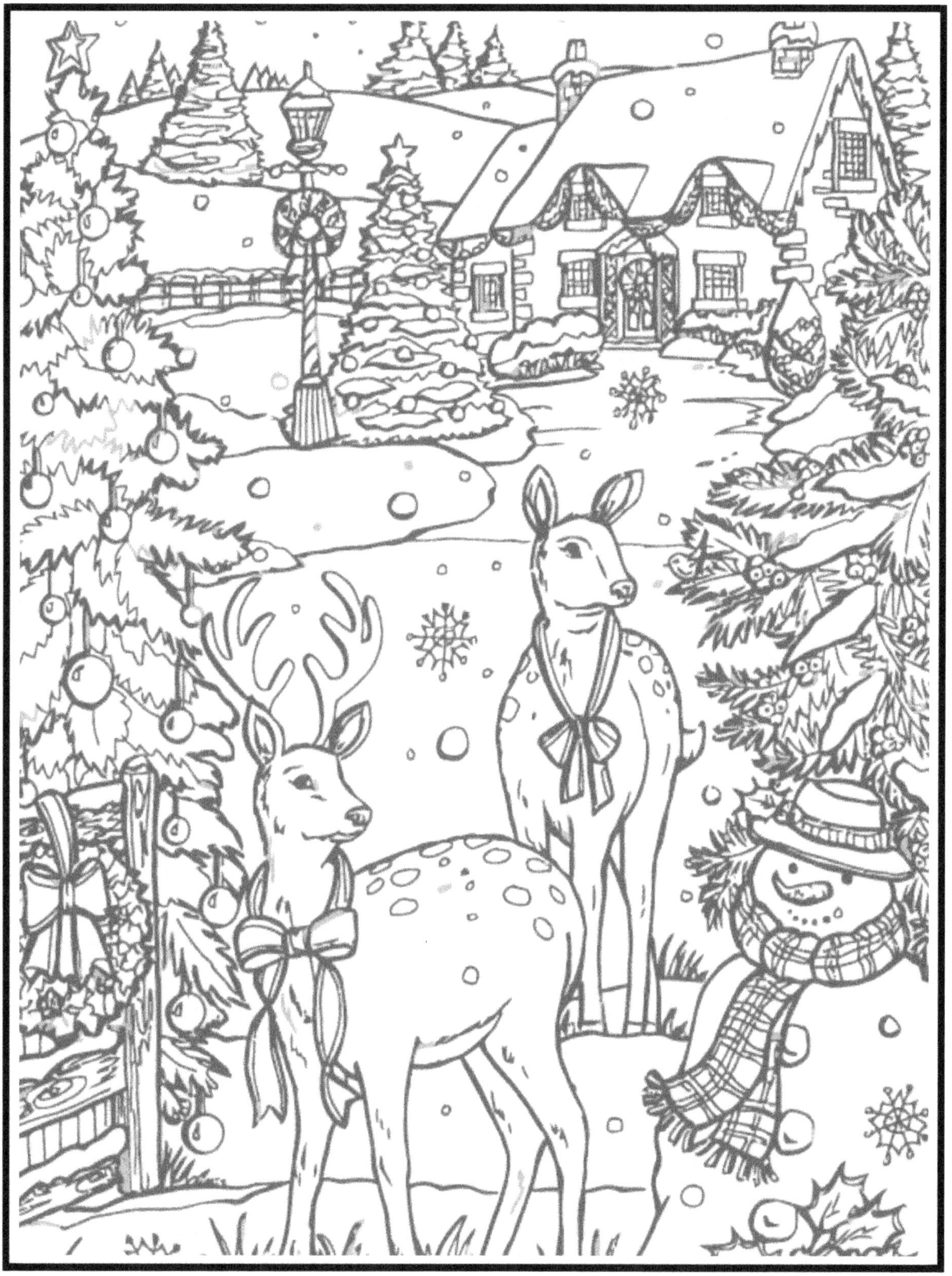

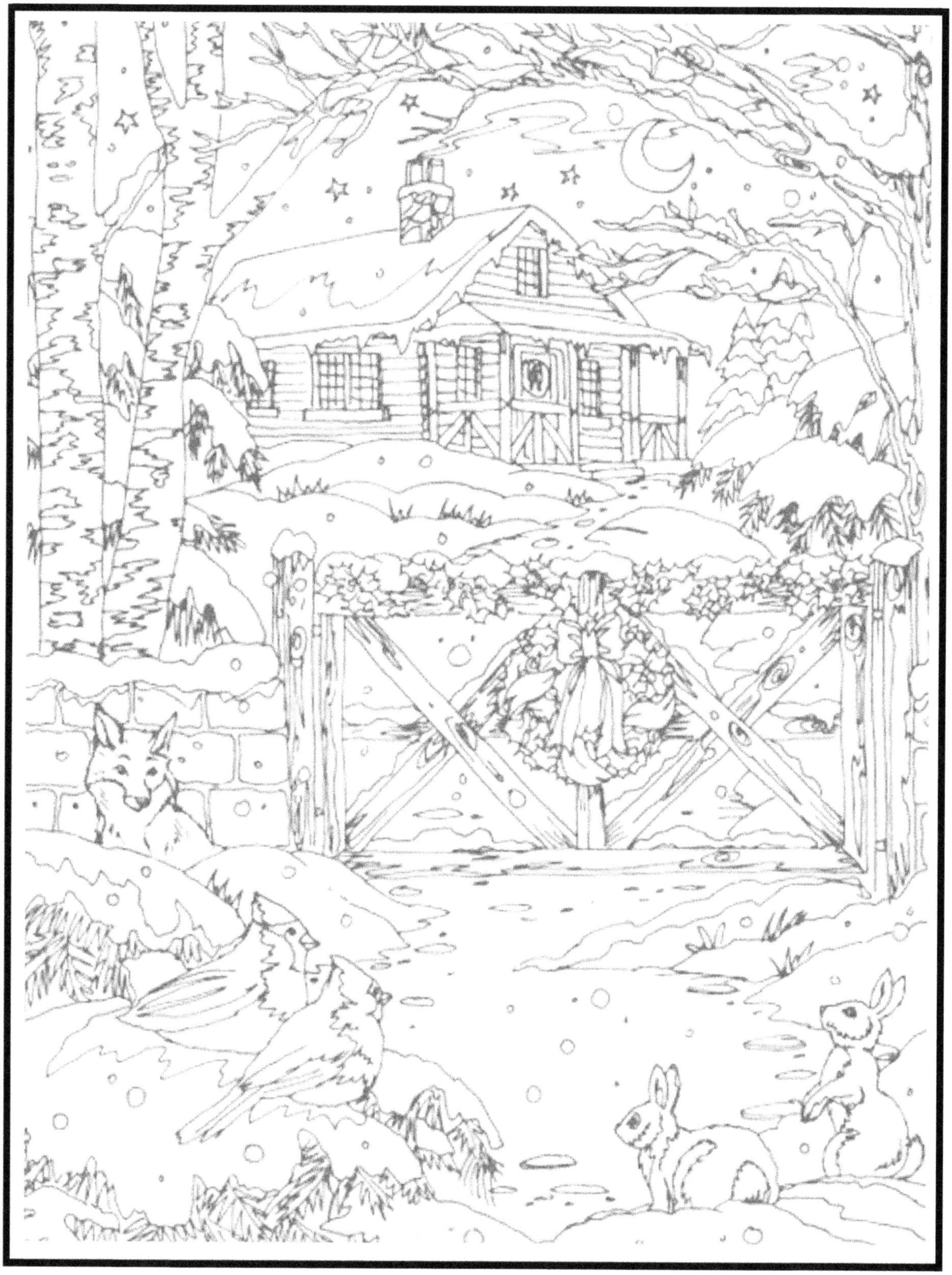

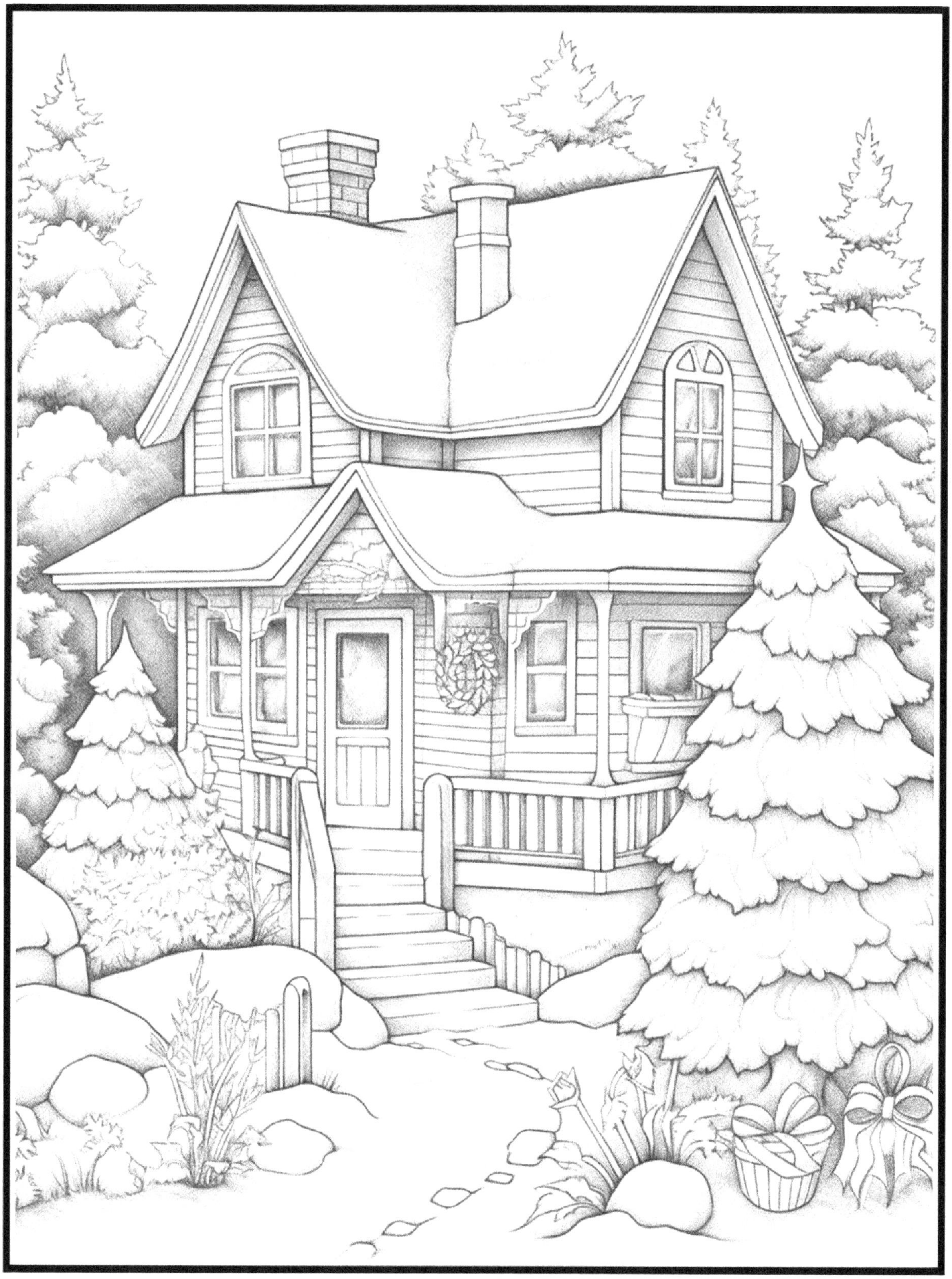

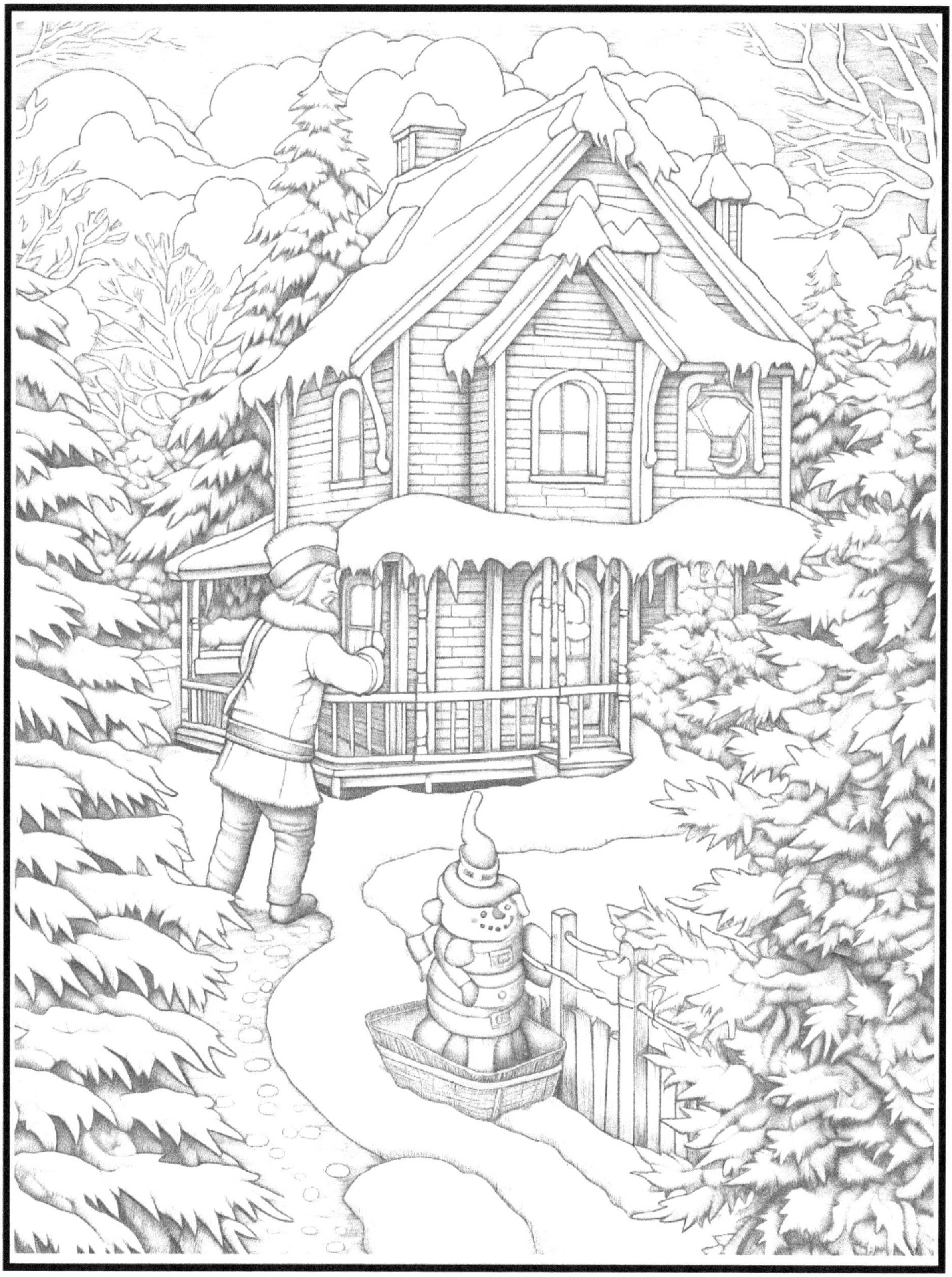

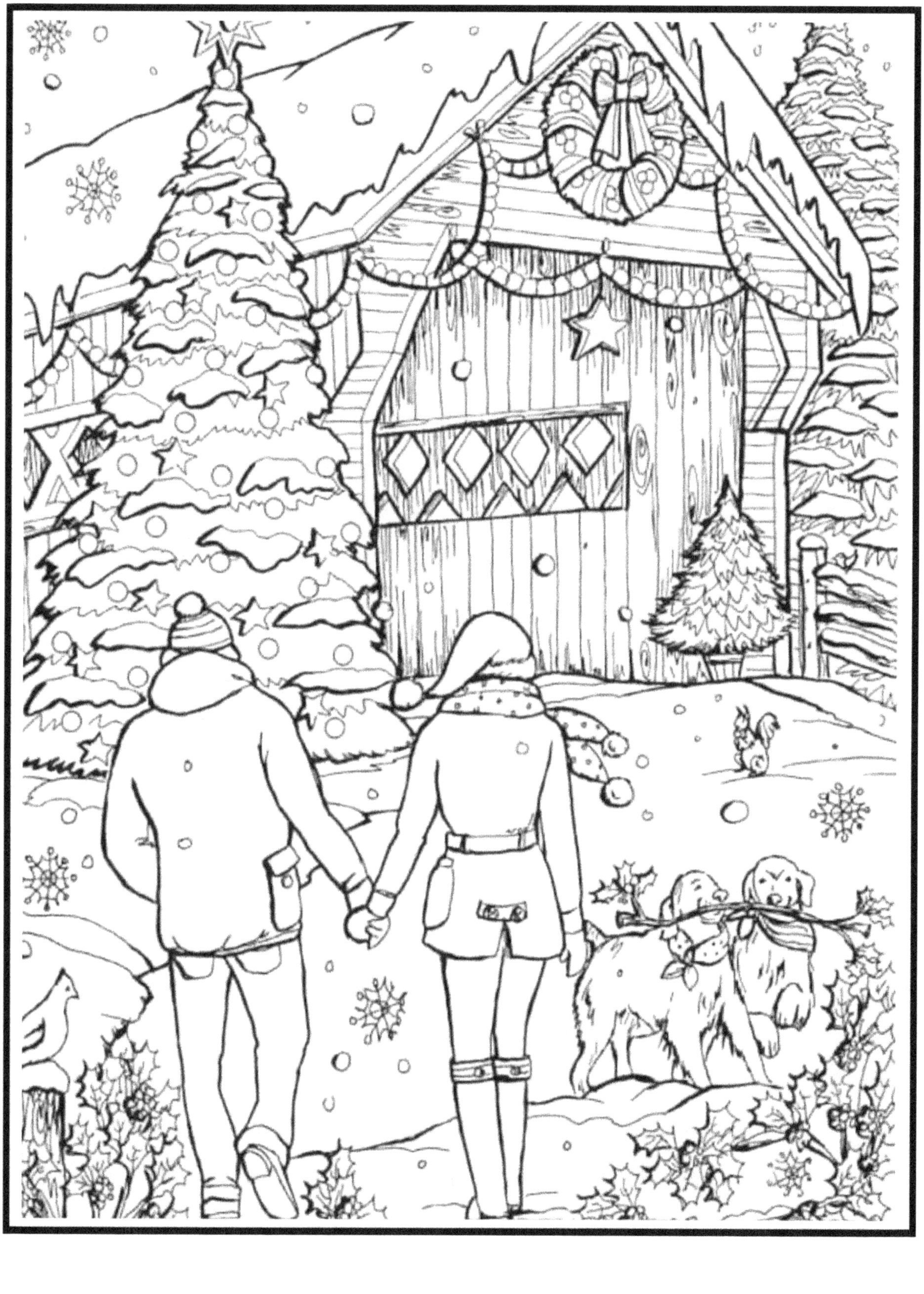

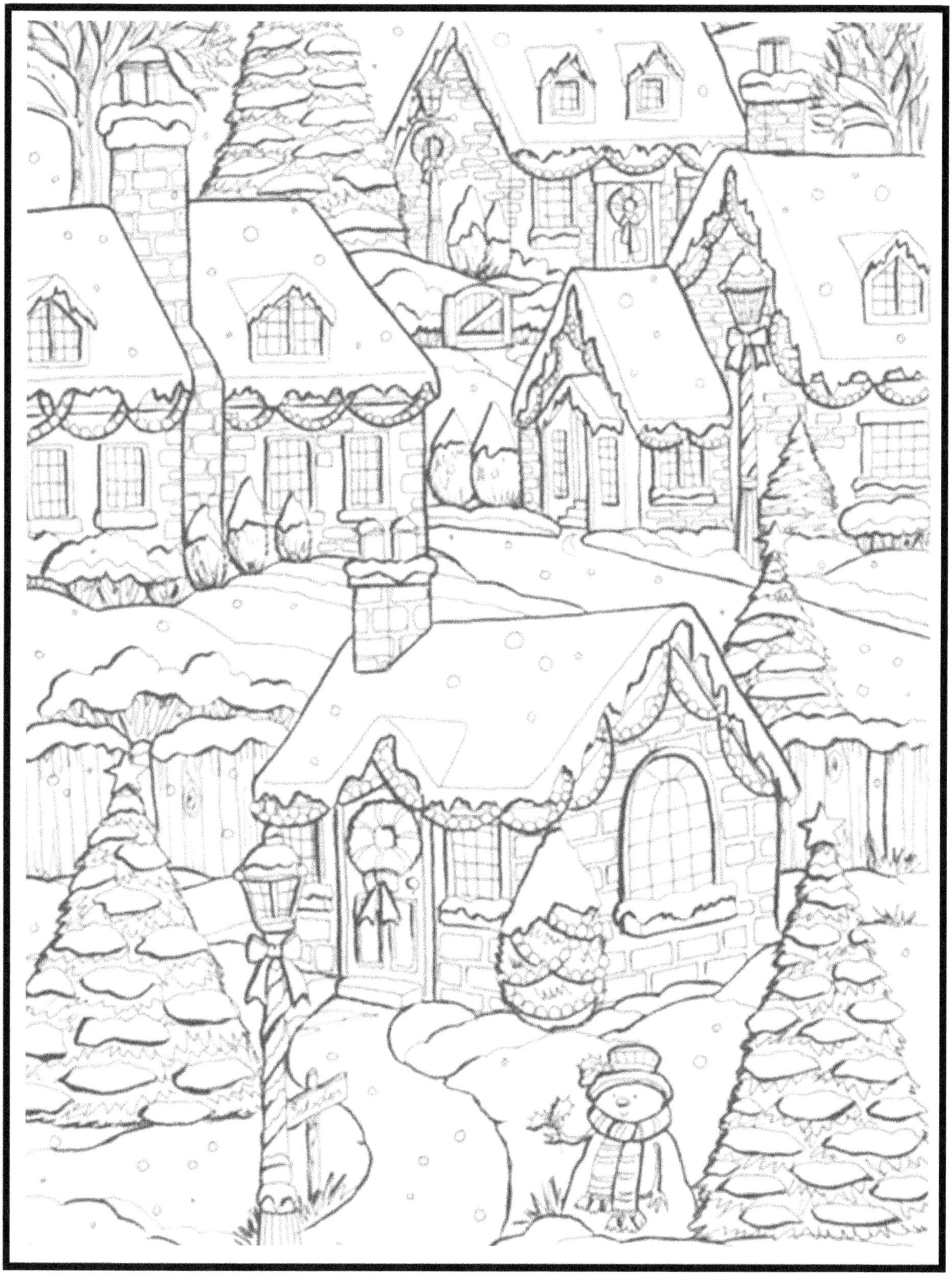

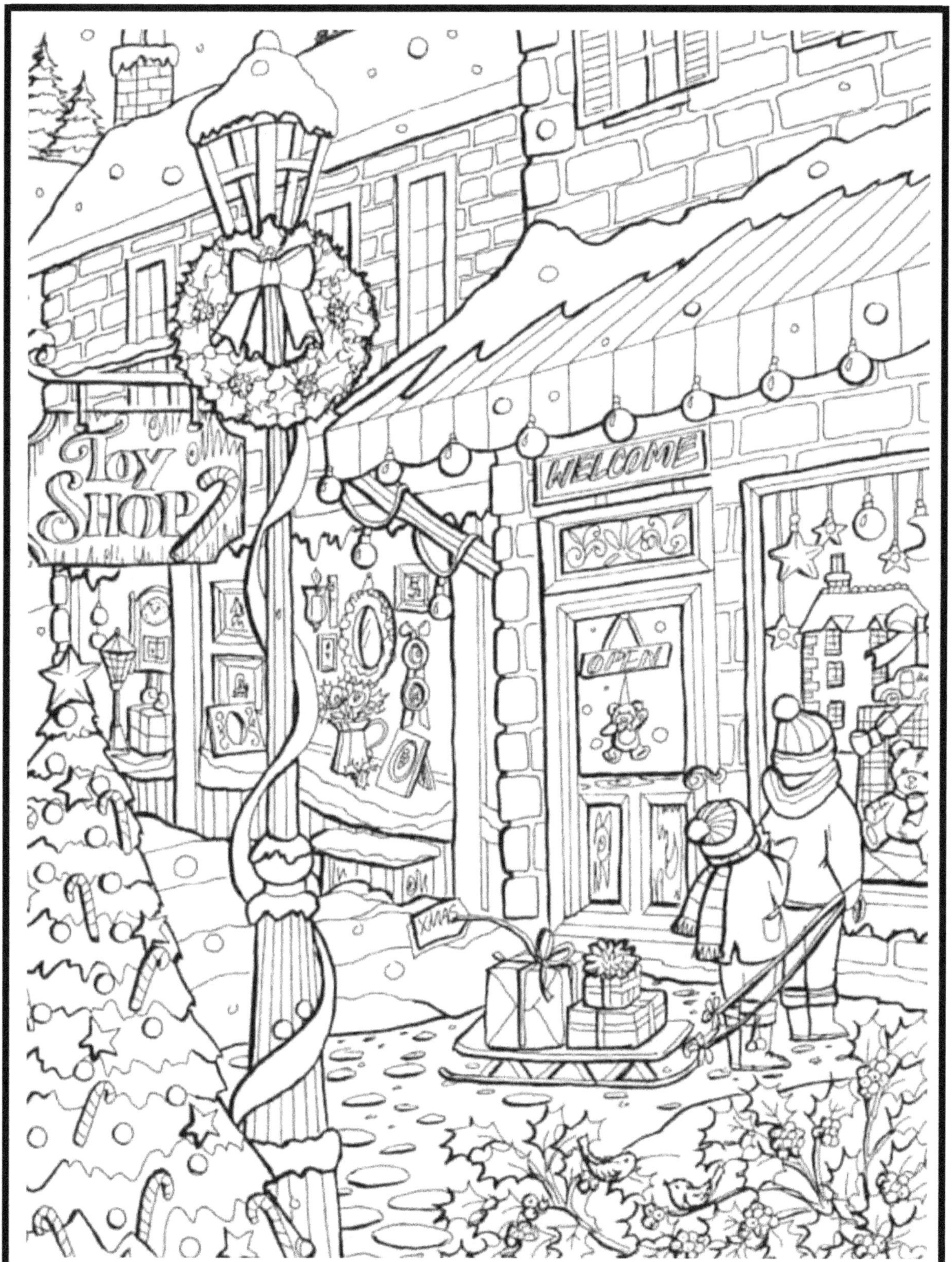

Toy
SHOP
WELCOME
OPEN
XMAS

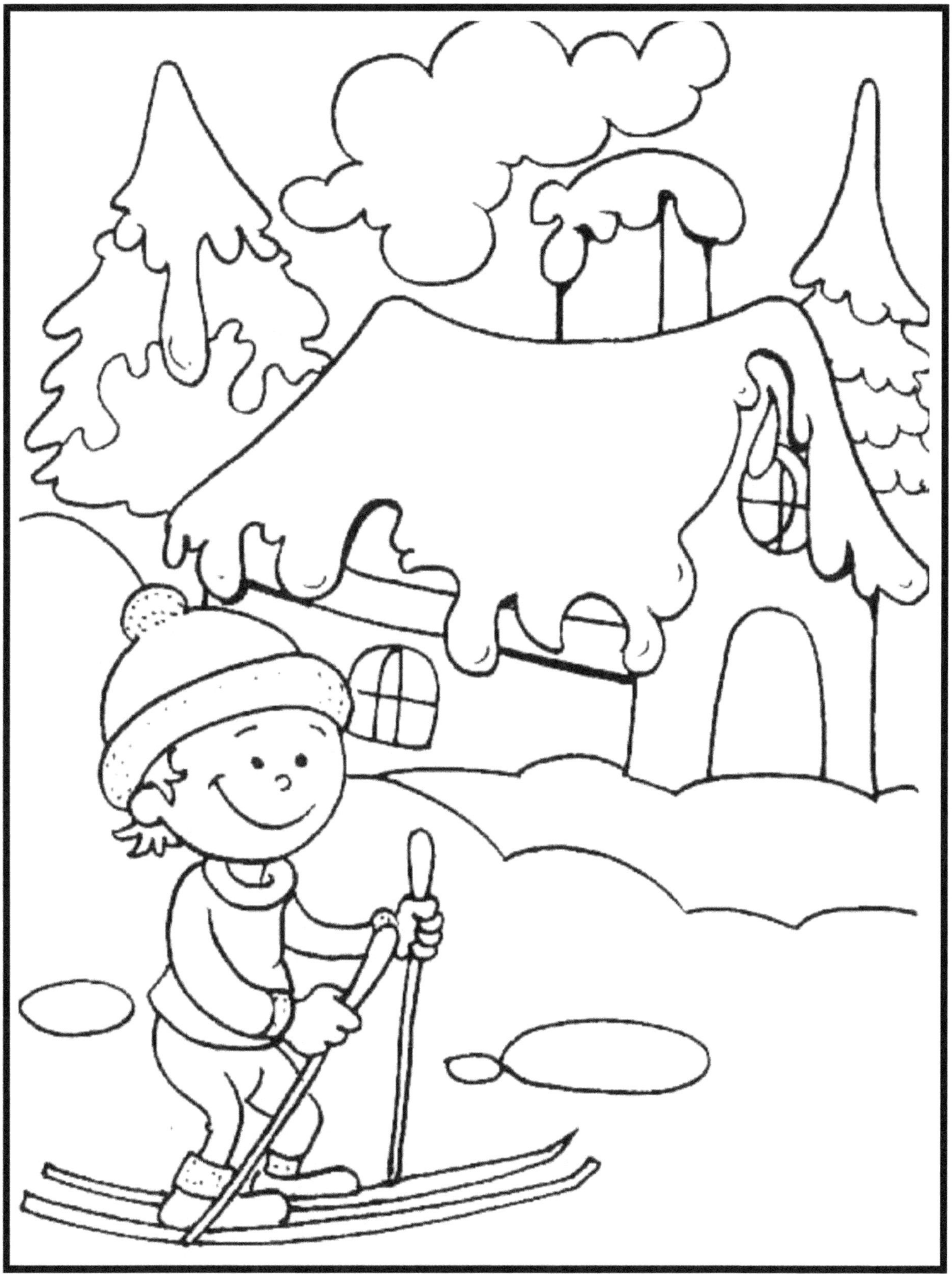

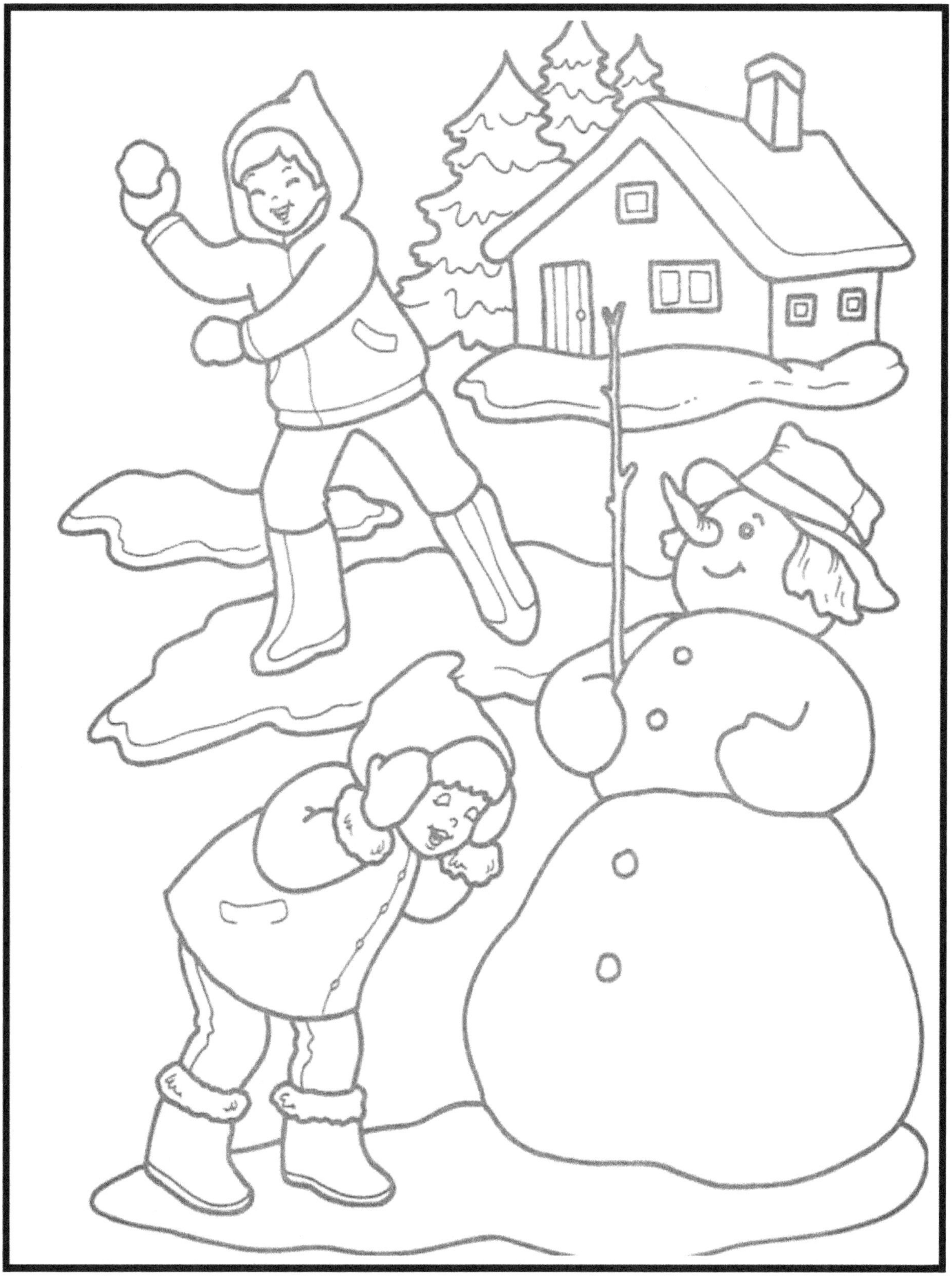

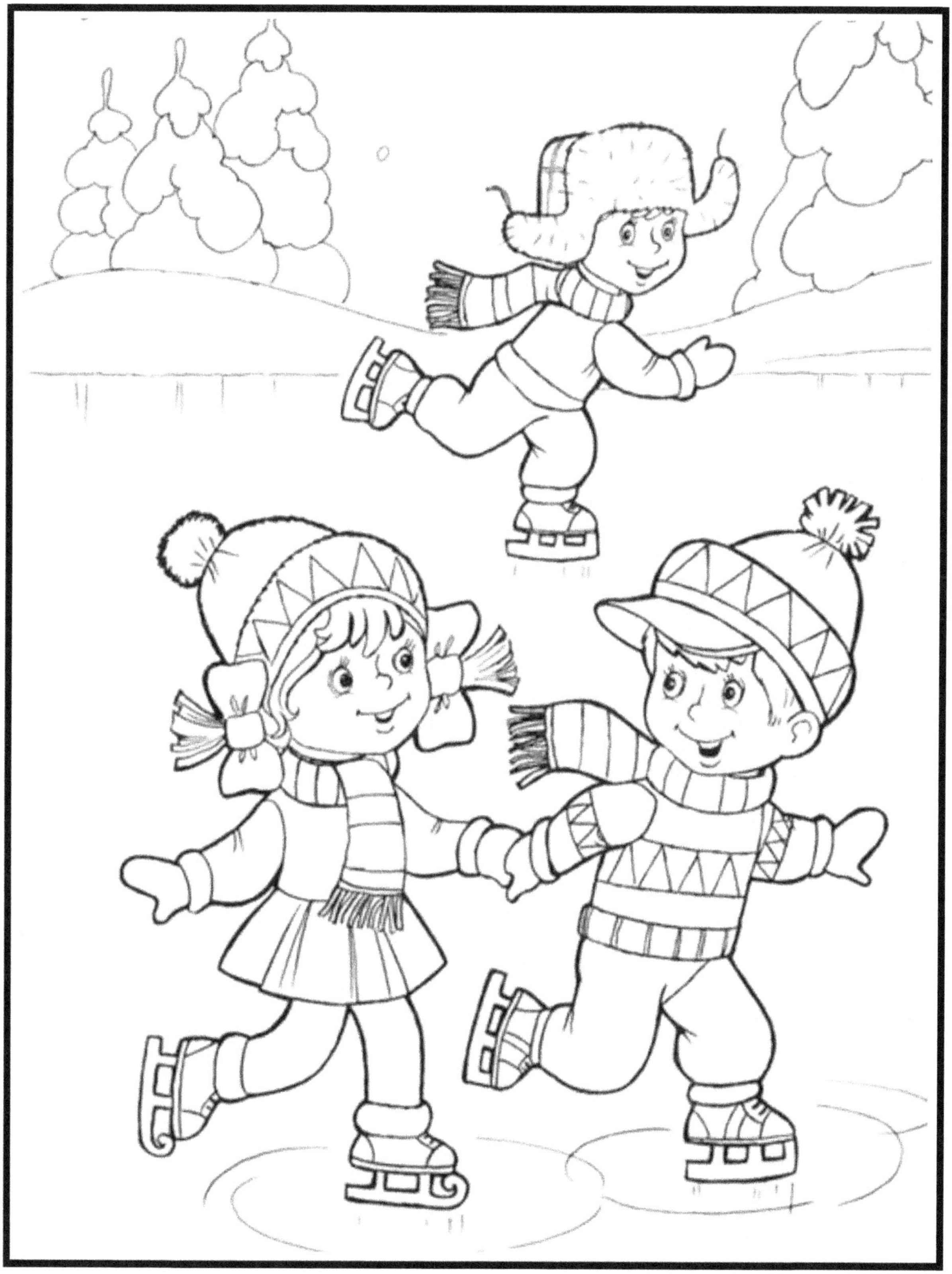

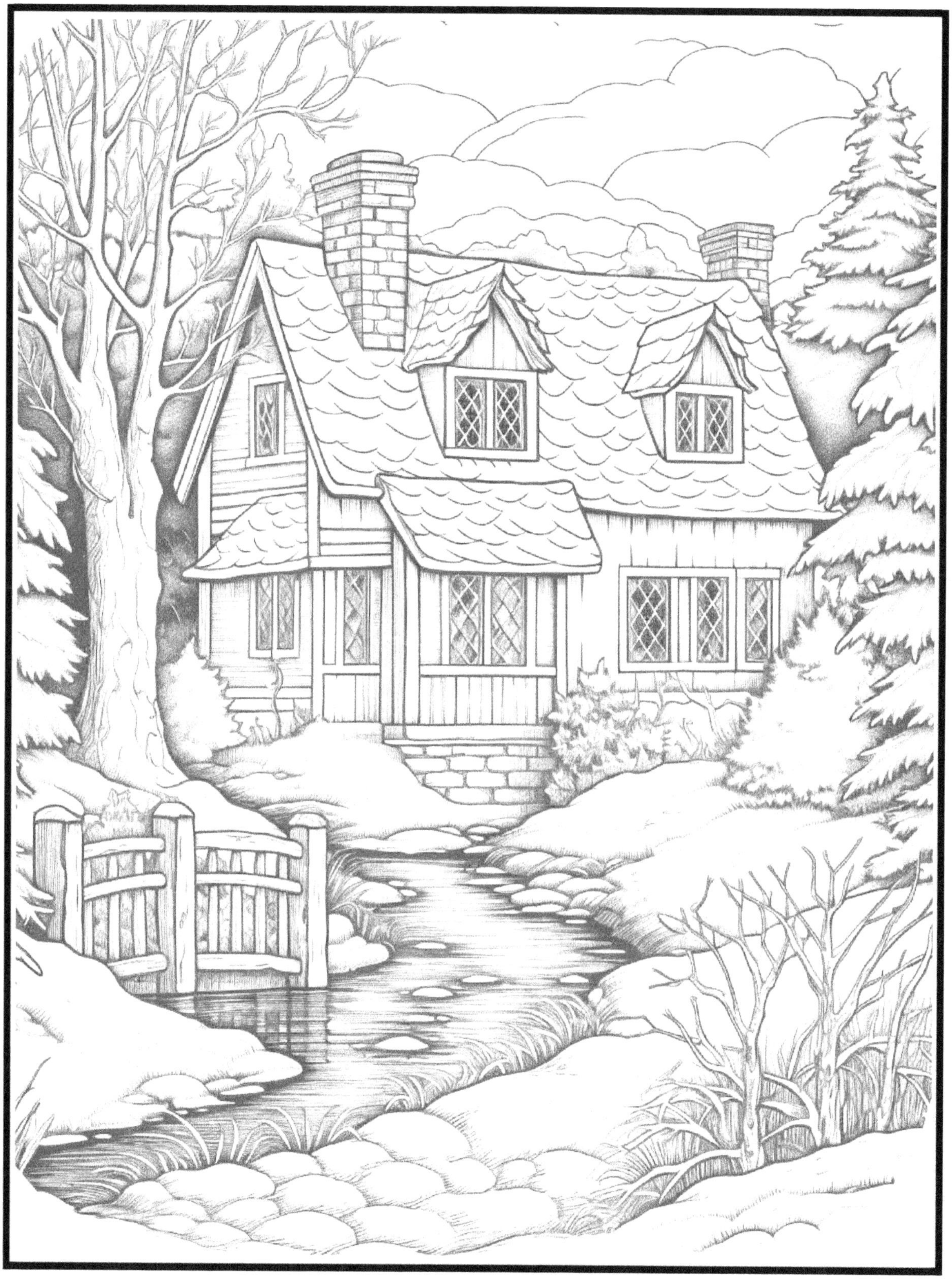

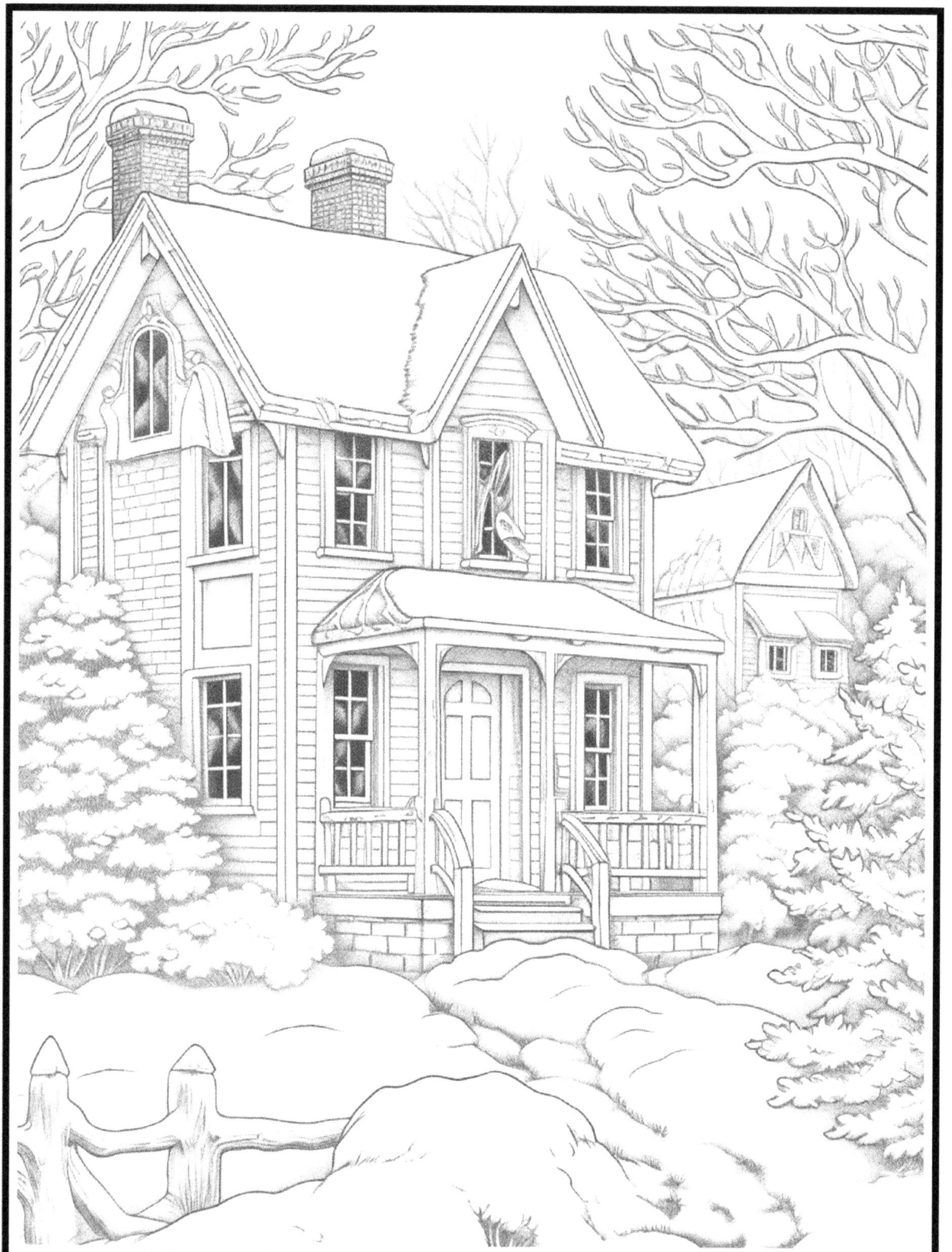

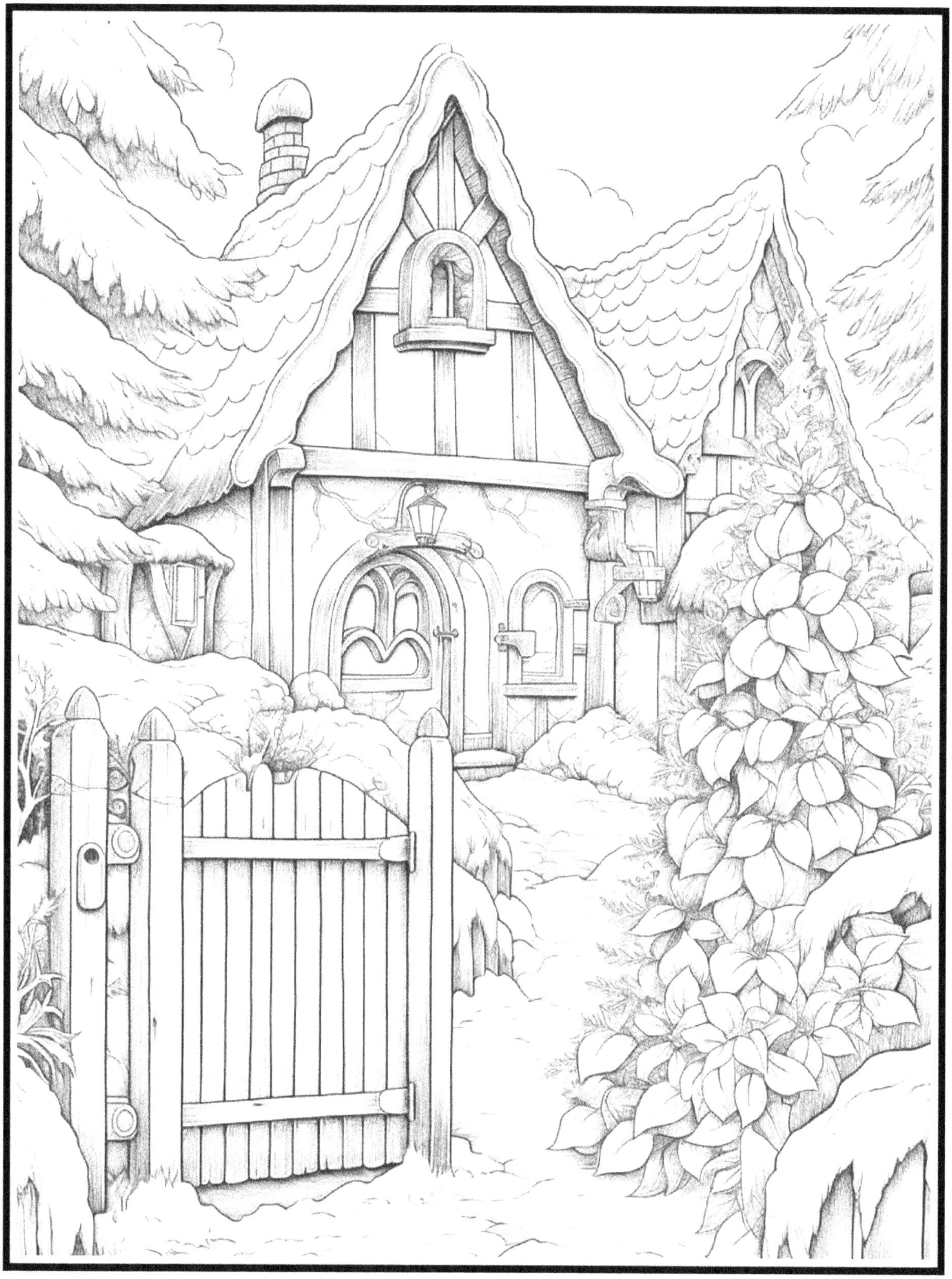

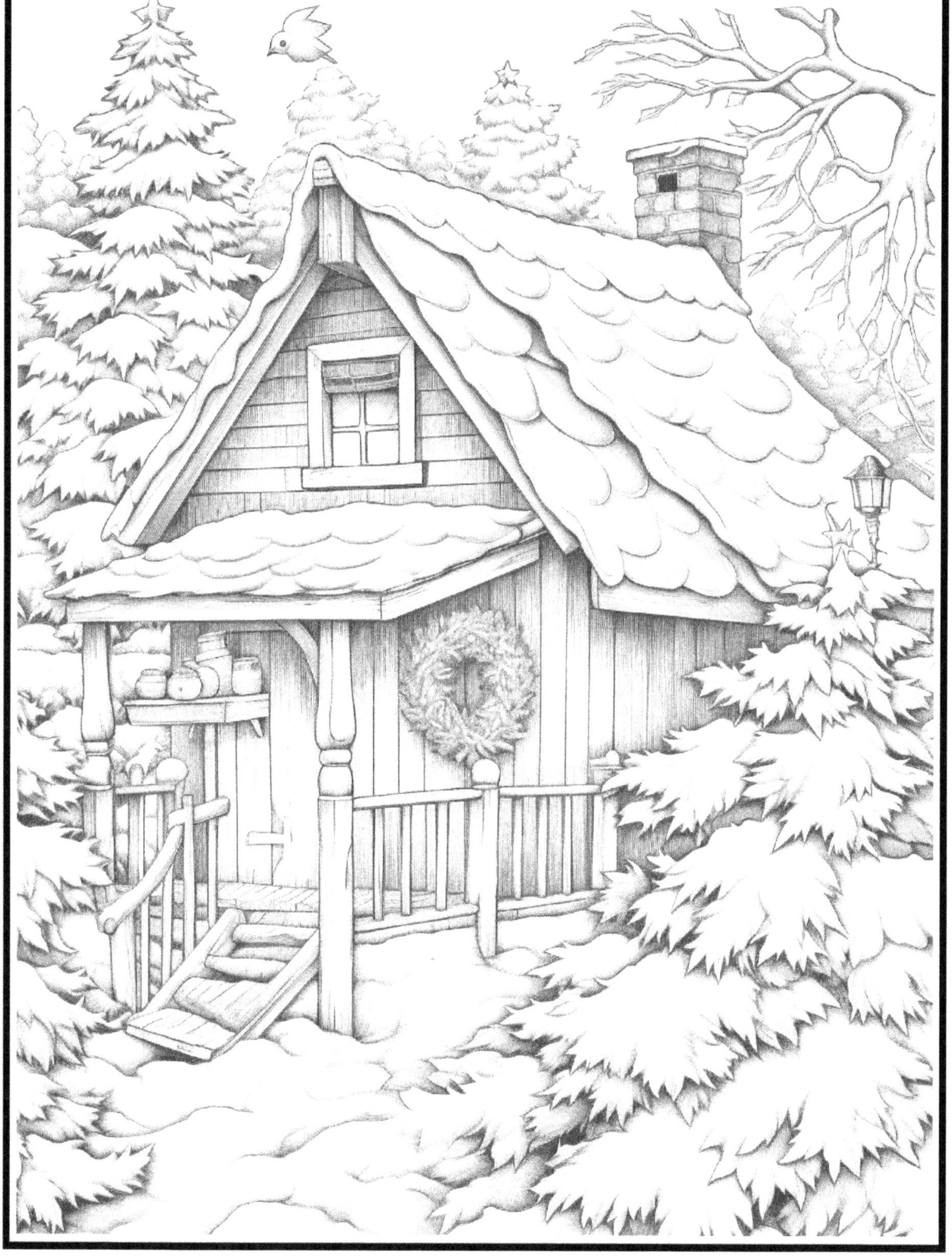

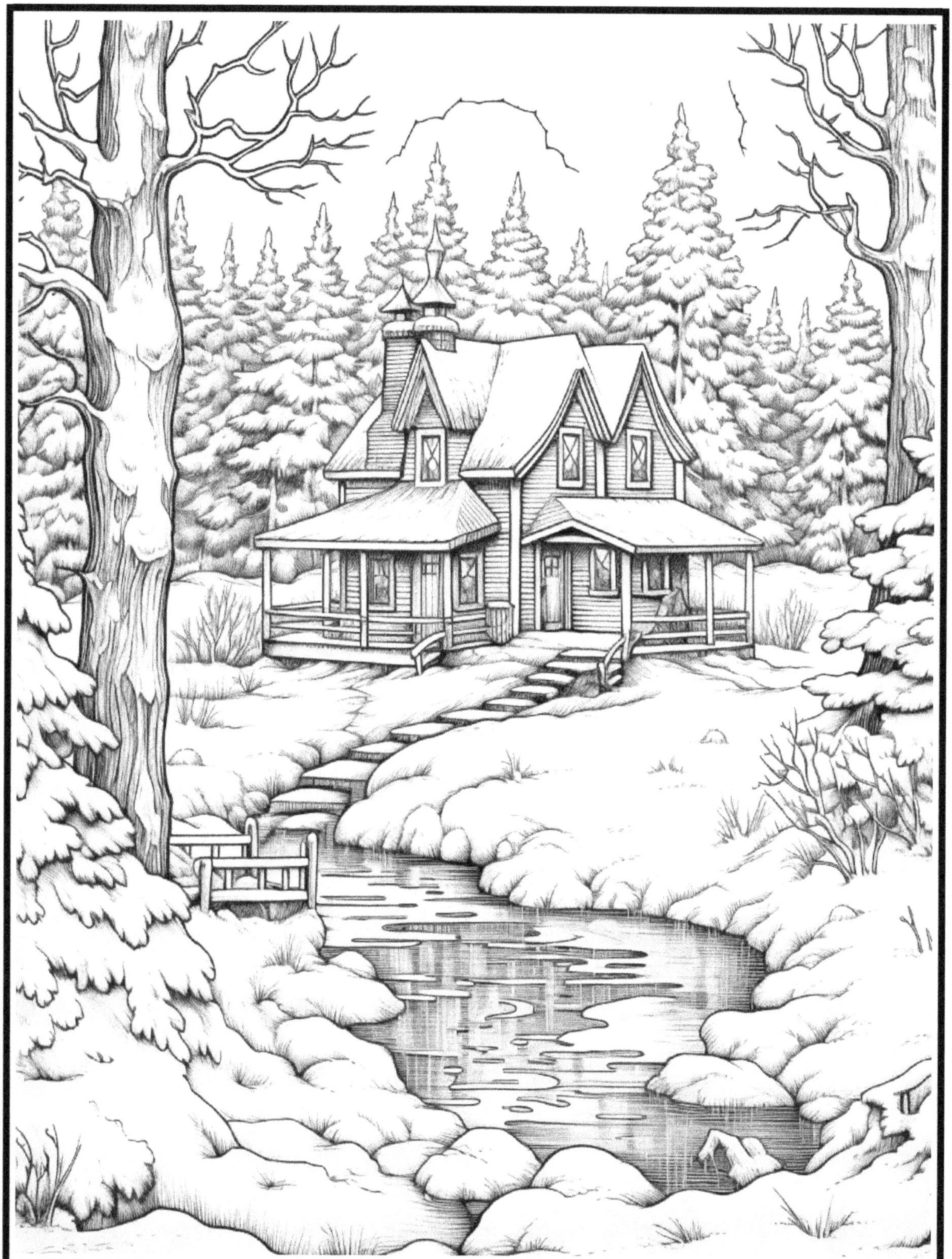

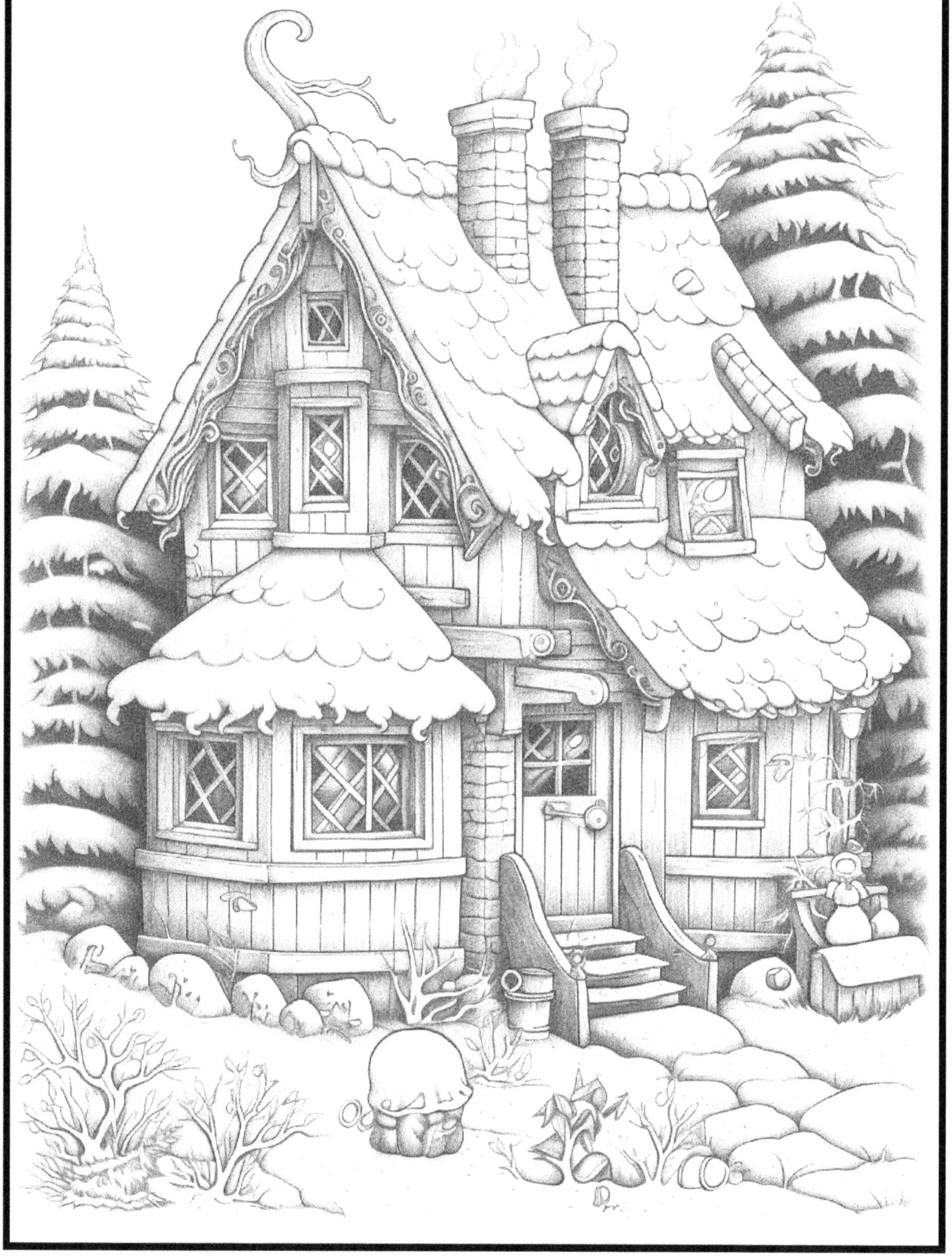

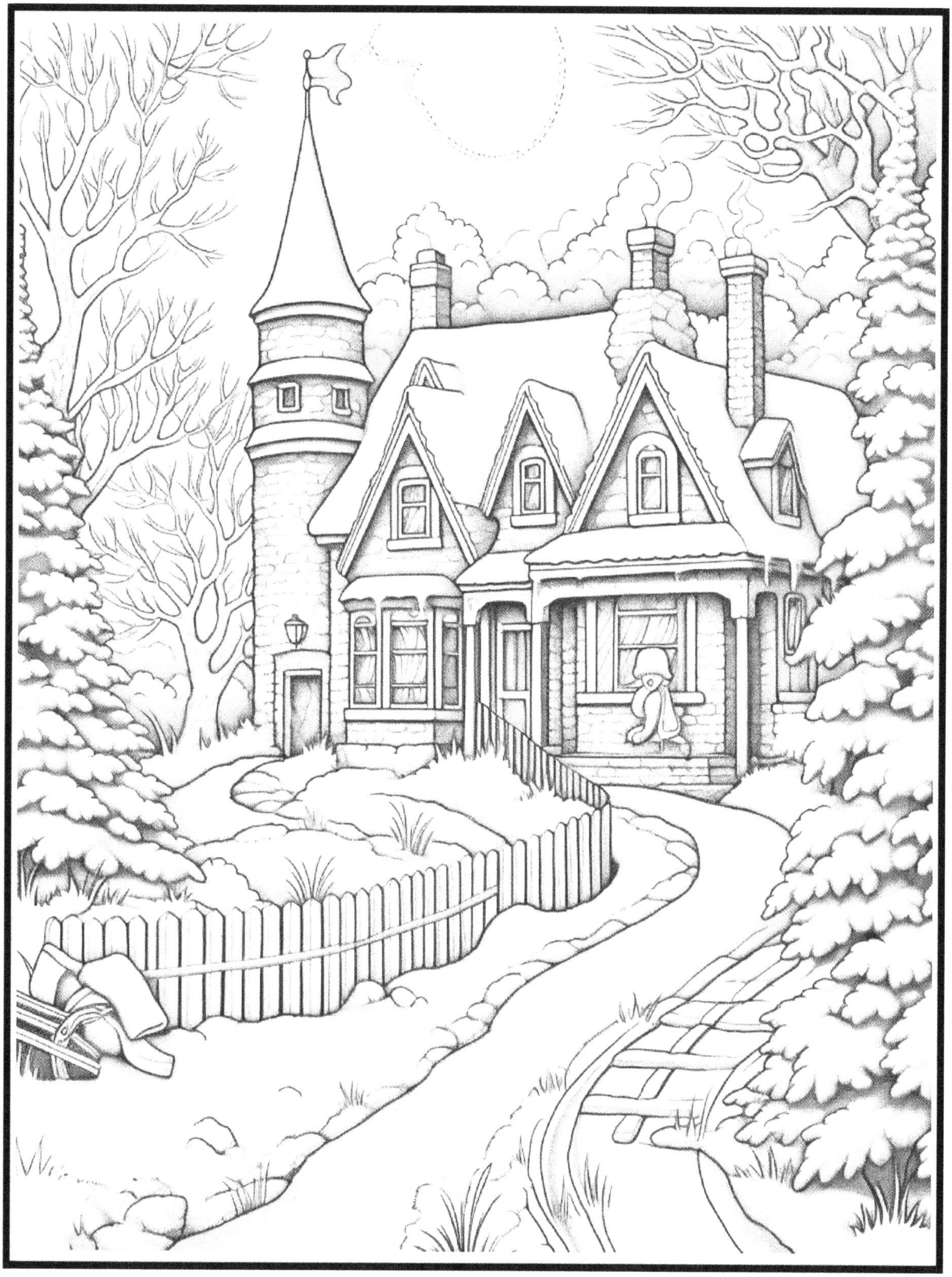

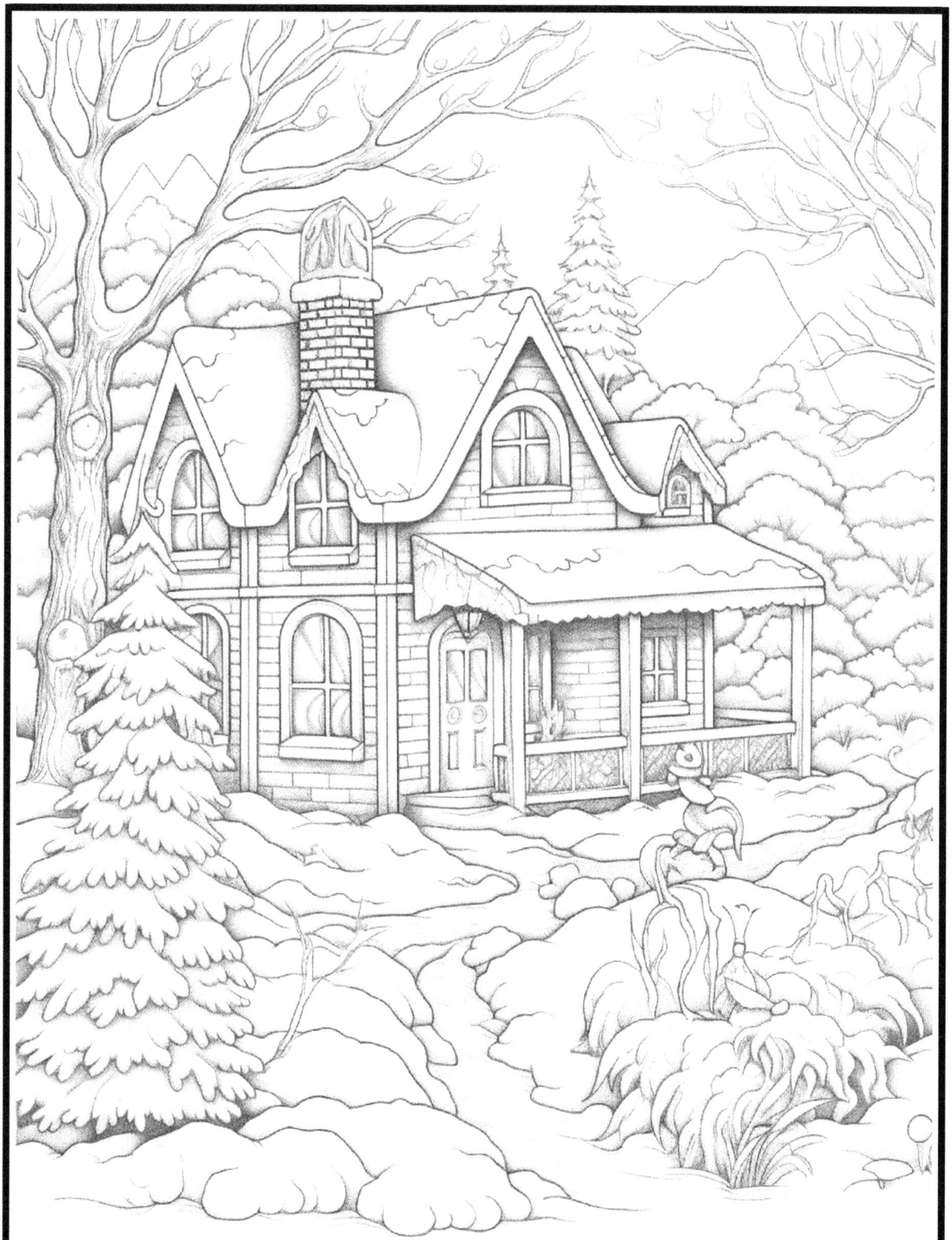

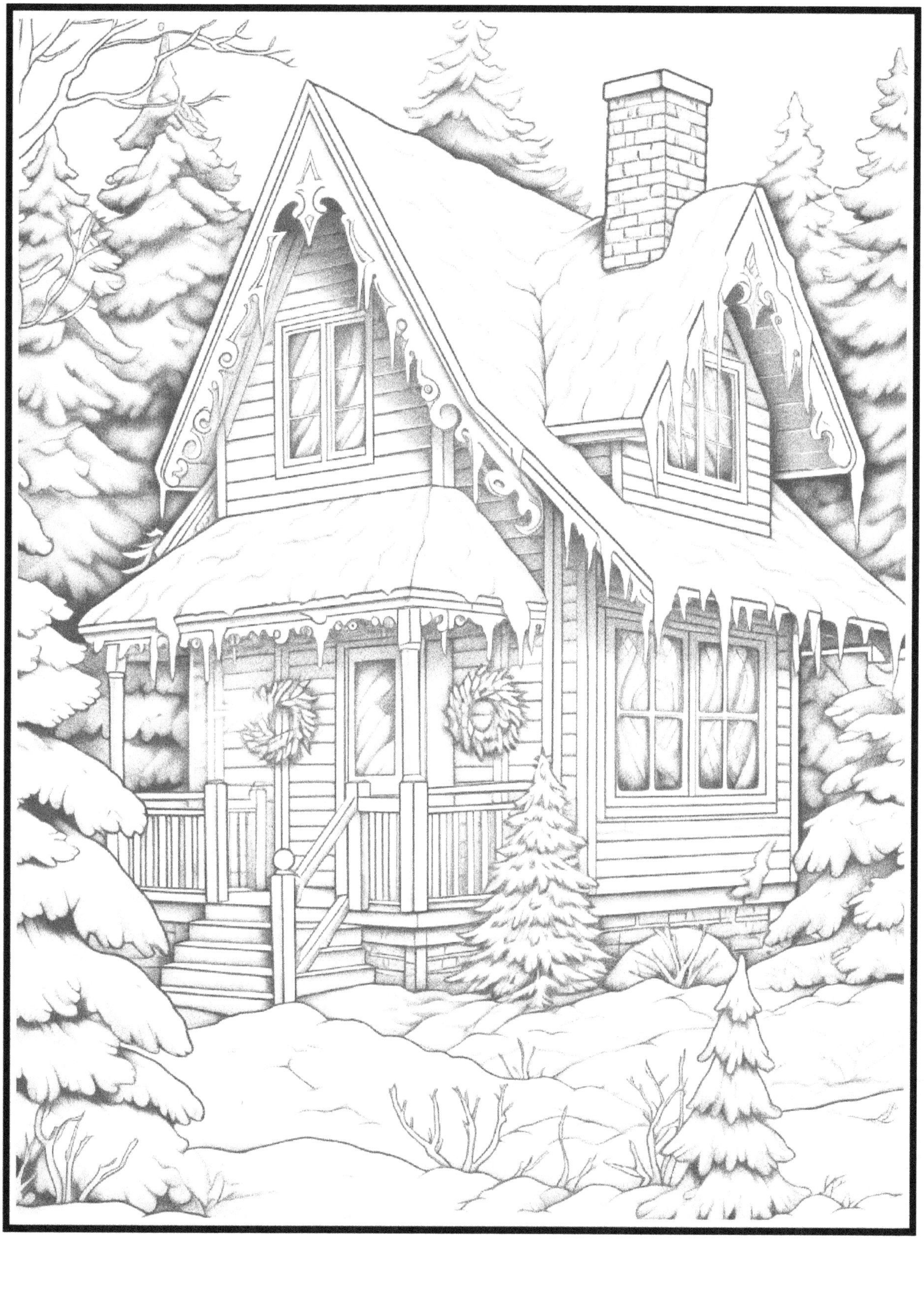

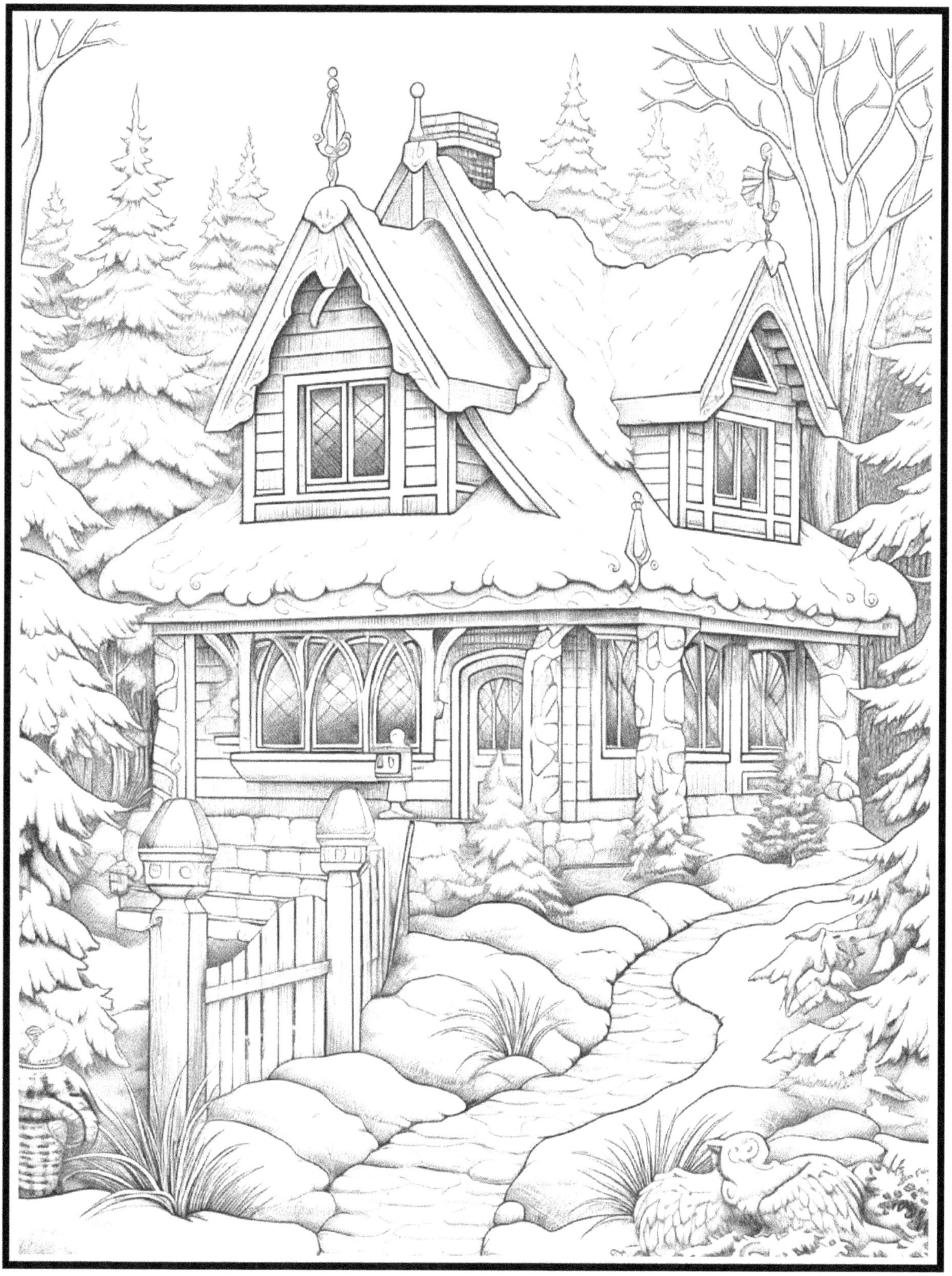

www.ingramcontent.com/pod-product-compliance
Lightning Source LLC
Chambersburg PA
CBHW081203290526
45796CB00010B/328
9798873971558